SOMETHING

NEW

UNDER

THE SUN

*Ancient
Wisdom for
Contemporary
Living*

RAY PRITCHARD

MOODY PRESS
CHICAGO

© 1998 by
RAY PRITCHARD

ISBN: 0-8024-8156-6

1 3 5 7 9 10 8 6 4 2

Printed in the United States of America

In honor of Mark and Ruth Wolery

CONTENTS

———— ✳ ————

ACKNOWLEDGMENTS

———— ✳ ————

Many friends prayed for me as I neared the end of this manuscript. I am especially grateful to the members of my Wednesday night Bible class for their insights as we journeyed through Ecclesiastes together. I learned at least as much from them as they did from me.

Special thanks to Jim Bell, Jim Vincent, and Linda Haskins of Moody Press. Bill Thrasher, general manager of Moody Press, had the vision of producing a trilogy of "wisdom" books for busy people. My thanks also to executive editor Greg Thornton, who suggested the study of Ecclesiastes as book two in this series.

Finally, I am keenly aware that I could not have written this book without the love and support of my wife, Marlene, and our three sons—Joshua, Mark, and Nicholas.

INTRODUCTION

———— ✳ ————

This book is not a commentary on Ecclesiastes. It may look that way, and it may be arranged that way, but it is something else entirely.

This is actually the second installment of a proposed trilogy of "wisdom books" for busy readers. Like many good ideas, this one didn't start out according to a predetermined plan. In 1997 I wrote a book called *The ABCs of Wisdom* based on the Book of Proverbs. I say "based on" because it wasn't a commentary either. It contains one hundred bite-sized nuggets of character-building truth based on some of the character qualities found in the Book of Proverbs, such as dependability, perseverance, punctuality, and compassion. I wrote about six hundred words on each topic and included a brief prayer and several questions to help readers do a bit of personal application.

When Greg Thornton of Moody Press asked if I would consider writing a sequel, I wondered what he had in mind. When he suggested Ecclesiastes, I took a deep breath, because it is as little known as Proverbs is well known. The ratio of regular readers of Proverbs versus Ecclesiastes is probably 1,000:1, which is odd since the two books rest side by side in the Old Testament.

Of course, there is an excellent reason for this. Proverbs is what it sounds like—short, pithy statements that are easy to understand (mostly) and often very challenging to put into practice. By contrast Ecclesiastes contains so many strange (some would say weird) statements that many people simply refuse to read the book.

Not long ago a friend told me (with great conviction) that Ecclesiastes was written by Solomon when he was in a backslidden spiritual condition. Having worked through the book myself, I can understand and partly sympathize with her sentiments. There are some statements in Ecclesiastes that are extremely hard to understand. I know that some people consider Ecclesiastes the most controversial book in the Bible.

However, I believe that when the whole context of the book is taken into account, it will be discovered that Solomon was a man of faith who leads his readers on a voyage through some of the backwater regions of life that we all think about but don't discuss in public. He isn't afraid to ask the hard questions and to admit when there are no easy answers. Since most of us like answers—simple, clear ones if possible—Solomon's words can sometimes seem very frustrating.

I would submit that there is nothing in Ecclesiastes that truly contradicts the rest of the Bible when we understand that Solomon is looking at life "under the sun"—that is, from a horizontal or earthly perspective. He simply wants to know, "What can we learn about the meaning of life by observing the world around us?" The answer is we can know a great deal, but many mysteries remain.

In the end I think Solomon is writing a kind of Old Testament apologetics in which he invites the secular person to join him on a search for ultimate truth.

I said this isn't a commentary, and very soon you will discover the truth of my words. What follows are bite-sized meditations on the meaning of life for busy people. Each one is based on a portion of the text—not as an exposition but rather touching on some of the underlying themes or else dealing with personal application. While King Solomon concludes wisely there is "nothing new under the sun" (Ecclesiastes 1:9), each reader will discover insights abounding—"something new under the sun"—in this inspired Bible book that chronicles a king's sweeping search for truth.

I've used the same format as *The ABCs of Wisdom* so that you can read each section "on the run" if necessary; reading one or two, putting the book down, and picking it up again later. Since Ecclesiastes contains many unusual sayings, I have added a feature called "More Light from God's Word." There you will find three Scripture passages from other Old and New Testament books. Please take time to read those passages because they give a broader perspective on the things Solomon wrote.

One final word. I hope you won't read this book straight through. You'll gain much more from it if you read one chapter of Ecclesiastes (about eight entries) a day, using it as a springboard for further Bible study and as a guide for thinking through some fundamental issues of the spiritual life. Or you can treat these as daily meditations; with one hundred entries, you have enough reading for twenty weeks, or almost five months (based on reading Monday through Friday).

For a generation desperately searching for reality—and not knowing where to find it—God wrote a book that sets our feet in the right direction. If you'd like to join Solomon on his journey to truth, Ecclesiastes is the place to begin.

One

---*---

SCOTT'S STORY

*The words of the Teacher, son of David, king in Jerusalem:
"Meaningless! Meaningless!" says the Teacher. "Utterly meaningless! Everything is meaningless."*

Ecclesiastes 1:1–2

Scott was only twenty-six years old when he died. Although he grew up in a Christian home, during his
teens and early twenties he went through a period of rebellion and spiritual searching. His life changed when the
doctors discovered a brain tumor. Surgery brought a brief
remission, but then the cancer returned.

As the months passed, his faith increased even as his
physical condition worsened. He began to seek the Lord
as never before. The Word of God became sweet to him.
He became bold in his witness, especially to his many
friends. He asked God to use him to reach others so that
he could point people to Christ no matter how long he
lived.

God answered the request. But several months later
Scott died.

During the funeral, his younger sister talked about
how much she loved him, how as a young girl she wanted
to be like him, and how exasperating he could be at
times. Then the cancer came. And she saw a difference so

profound that it changed everything. Her brother, she said, had figured out what life is all about. Then she said this: "Life is nothing without God." Scott had shown her that it doesn't matter how long you live or how much money you have or even how well you do in your career. His faith at the end spoke one simple message: Life is nothing without God.

When I stood up to deliver the message a few minutes later, I didn't have to say very much. I simply repeated what she said one more time: *Life is nothing without God.*

I then made this simple application. If you live for eighty years but don't discover that truth, you've missed the very reason for your own existence. If you should earn a million dollars—ten million dollars—and have hundreds of friends and the praise of your contemporaries, if you have all that but don't figure out this basic truth, you're still in spiritual kindergarten.

Life is nothing without God. Everything else is just details. Your career, your education, your degrees, your money, your fame, your accomplishments, your long-range goals, your dreams, your possessions, your friendships—they're all just details. If you don't figure out that God is the central truth of the universe, you will spend your days mired in details, drifting along with no clear purpose. That's the ultimate "vanity" that causes life to be meaningless.

Have you discovered what life is all about? Life is nothing without God. Everything else is just details.

O God, show me what life is all about so that I won't waste my years on things that don't really matter. Amen.

SHINING THE LIGHT

* Was Solomon a pessimist, an optimist, or a realist? Which of those three words describes you best?

* Do you agree that "life is nothing without God"?

MORE LIGHT FROM GOD'S WORD
Read Psalm 90:1–2; John 1:3; and Romans 11:30–33.

Two

---------- ✳ ----------

THE ULTIMATE QUESTION

*What does man gain from all his labor at which he toils un-
der the sun?*

Ecclesiastes 1:3

Solomon's question in verse 3 begs for an answer. Mine
goes like this: What you gain from your labor depends
on why you are doing it. There is a huge difference between living for your career and being sent on a mission.
The Bible never talks about having a career. You'll never
find the word in the Bible. Having a career is not a biblical issue. Having a mission is.

It is not that Christians don't have careers. We do.
Some of us are painters, some are doctors, some are computer scientists, some are bankers, some are nurses, some
are teachers, and some are writers. And some are home-
makers and mothers (an honorable and often overlooked
career). But the difference is this: The people of the world
live for their careers; the people of God don't.

When your career is central in your life, then you are
career-driven and career-minded as you climb the career
ladder. You take a job and leave it two years later because
it's "a good career move." You break all the significant relationships in one place and move across the country because your career demands it. Everything is calculated to

get you someday to that elusive place called "the top." When you get there, your career will be complete and the world will applaud your achievements.

I am suggesting that being career-minded in this sense is precisely what Jesus meant when He said, "Whoever wants to save his life will lose it" (Mark 8:35). Your career may well keep you from fulfilling your mission in life, and your mission may never make much sense as a career.

Your career is the answer to the question, "What do you do for a living?"

Your mission is the answer to the question, "Why did God put you here on the earth?"

If you are just here to eat, sleep, go to college, get a degree, get married, get a job, have some children, climb the ladder, make some money, buy a summer home, retire gracefully, grow old and die . . . then what's the big deal? All of that is OK, but if that's all there is to life, then you are really no different from the pagans who don't even believe in God.

It's nice to have a career; it's far better to be on a mission for God.

Ask yourself, Did Jesus have a career? No, He had a mission from God to be the Savior of the world. Nothing He did makes sense from a career point of view. Being crucified is not a good career move. Yet by His death, He reconciled the world to God. Was He a success or a failure?

Eternal God, You alone give meaning to life. Give me such confidence in Your Son that I might follow in His steps forever. Amen.

—✳—

SHINING THE LIGHT

✳ What is your personal definition of success?

✳ If you were to die today, would you regard your life as having been a success from God's point of view? If the answer is no, what needs to change before you can answer yes?

—✳—

MORE LIGHT FROM GOD'S WORD
Read Joshua 1:8; Job 20:20–22; and Mark 8:36.

Three

THE TREADMILL

Generations come and generations go, but the earth remains forever. The sun rises and the sun sets, and hurries back to where it rises. The wind blows to the south and turns to the north; round and round it goes, ever returning on its course. All streams flow into the sea, yet the sea is never full. To the place the streams come from, there they return again. All things are wearisome, more than one can say. The eye never has enough of seeing, nor the ear its fill of hearing.

Ecclesiastes 1:4–8

Generations come and generations go." In 1517 Martin Luther ignited the Protestant Reformation when he nailed his Ninety-five Theses to the door of the church in Wittenberg, Germany. That same year Bernard Gilpin was born. He became an English church leader who worked for social reform. He died in 1583, the same year that Simon Episcopius was born. He became a leader of the Dutch church and took part in the Remonstrance of 1610. He died in 1643, the same year that Solomon Stoddard was born. He was the first librarian of Harvard College and the grandfather of Jonathan Edwards. He died in 1729, the same year that Catherine the Great was born. She was Empress of Russia and brought the ideas of the Enlightenment to the Russian Empire. She died in

1796, the same year that Horace Mann was born. We remember him as the founder of free public education in the United States. He died in 1859, the year that John Dewey was born. He became a controversial figure for theories regarding the education of children and teenagers. He died in 1952, the same year that I was born.

That's seven generations spanning 435 years. And I, well, I've done nothing comparable to any of those important figures. But I have one great advantage over them. They're dead and I'm alive. But I will pass off the scene eventually, and someone (many people, to be precise) will be born on the very day I die.

Life is truly short and transitory. Most of us have never heard of the first two names on the list—Gilpin and Episcopius. Theology students might know about Solomon Stoddard. Probably everyone has at least heard of Catherine the Great, Horace Mann, and John Dewey. But all the names grow fainter by the day, dusty remnants of the past. And so, sooner than I prefer, my name will join theirs, and generations will rise up and never know I existed. Surely this is the height of futility.

Isaac Watts said it well: "Time, like an ever-rolling stream, bears all its sons away; they fly, forgotten, as a dream dies at the opening day." Those lines from "O God, Our Help in Ages Past" remind us that only God can give our lives significance. Without Him we are here today, gone tomorrow, and eventually forgotten.

Father, You are from everlasting to everlasting. When the earth itself passes away, You will remain forever. I believe that You are eternal and that Your Son is the light of the world. Amen.

——✳——

SHINING THE LIGHT

✴ How many generations can you count on your own family tree?

✴ How long do you expect to be remembered after you die?

✴ What are you doing today that will matter one hundred years from now?

——✳——

MORE LIGHT FROM GOD'S WORD

Read Isaiah 40:7–8; John 8:58; and Ephesians 1:10–13.

Four

------------ ✳ ------------

RAINBOWS, IF YOU SEE THEM

What has been will be again, what has been done will be done again; there is nothing new under the sun. Is there anything of which one can say, "Look! This is something new"? It was here already, long ago; it was here before our time.

Ecclesiastes 1:9–10

Commentators on Ecclesiastes remark that this early portion of the book deals with the "round of life." Derek Kidner points out that life is like a long journey to nowhere in particular. We get up, go to work, come home, eat supper, watch TV, and go to bed. Tomorrow we get up and repeat the routine. This is the story of life "under the sun."

Solomon's observation happens to be correct. Perhaps 99 percent of life is ordinary. In the words of the crusty curmudgeon Andy Rooney, "For most of life, nothing wonderful happens." He goes on to say, in one of his commentaries on daily living, that if you can't find happiness in things like having a cup of coffee with your wife or sitting down to a meal with family and friends, then you're probably not going to be very happy. If you sit around dreaming about winning the big contract or wondering when the Yankees are going to make you their starting pitcher, you're going to spend most of your days waiting for something that isn't going to happen.

Meanwhile the sun will rise tomorrow and you won't see it. A friend will say hello and it won't matter, your children will giggle but you won't smile, the roses will bloom, white snow will cover the front yard, your husband will offer to rub your back, the choir will sing your favorite hymn—and because it's ordinary or you've seen it before or heard it before or done it before, and because you're dreaming of the future, you'll miss it altogether.

Here's an old story from the comic strip "Peanuts." Lucy is down on her knees, looking intently at something on the ground when Charlie Brown comes along. She says, "I've been watching these bugs, Charlie Brown. You see, this one bug here is about to leave home. He's been saying good-bye to all his friends. Suddenly, this little girl bug comes running up and tries to persuade him not to leave." Charlie Brown looks up with an amazed and puzzled look on his face. Lucy concludes, "If you're going to be a good bug-watcher, you have to have lots of imagination."

Lucy is right, of course. What you see is what you want to see. Some people look at life and see nothing but bugs. Other people see a love story.

It's true that there is "nothing new under the sun." But that doesn't mean life isn't worth living. The world is filled with rainbows for those who have eyes to see them.

Father, I pray for eyes to see the rainbows all around me. Amen.

27

— ✳ —

SHINING THE LIGHT

* How do you reconcile the parade of human progress with the truth that there is nothing new under the sun?

* Are you more likely to see bugs or a love story?

* How does Jesus Christ create something "new" in your life?

— ✳ —

MORE LIGHT FROM GOD'S WORD

Read Jeremiah 31:31–34; 2 Corinthians 5:17; and Revelation 21:5.

------------ ✳ ------------

Five

FADED PHOTOGRAPHS

*There is no remembrance of men of old, and even those who
are yet to come will not be remembered by those who follow.*
Ecclesiastes 1:11

There is good news and bad news in Ecclesiastes 1:11.
The good news is for those people who worry about
what others think about them. In the end no one will
think about you at all. The bad news is for those who
seek some kind of temporal immortality. In the end no
one will think about you at all.

If you doubt my words, check out any graveyard. See
how many names you recognize. Several years ago I spent
two hours on a cemetery walk sponsored by our local historical society. Most people, I suppose, would find the
idea of touring a cemetery somewhat depressing, but I
found it fascinating. Graveyards have a story to tell for
those who care to listen.

Evangelist Billy Sunday is buried in this cemetery.
Between 1900 and 1930 he traveled from city to city,
preaching to hundreds of thousands in huge tents and
tabernacles, calling the unconverted to "hit the sawdust
trail." He was the Billy Graham before Billy Graham.
Chiseled in marble on his tomb are these words from 2
Timothy 4:7, "I have fought the good fight, I have fin-

ished the course, I have kept the faith" (NASB).

Along the way we saw the graves of many of the founders of this area. A Civil War general is buried there, along with Ernest Hemingway's parents.

At one point our guide showed us a monument with two names on it. "Dr.—— usually listens in to make sure we get our facts right," she said. I thought she meant that metaphorically, as if the good doctor somehow tuned in from the Great Beyond. But, no, she meant it literally. The doctor and his wife are still alive and well. They have already placed their own monument in the cemetery, planning to occupy the ground beneath it sometime in the future.

We stopped longest at the memorial to the Haymarket martyrs. A professor from the University of Illinois told us the gripping story of the 1886 rally in Haymarket Square, the first dynamite bomb in American history, the crooked trial that followed, the hanging of six men, and the 500,000 people who lined the streets to watch the funeral procession.

Many things run through the mind while visiting a cemetery at twilight. Things are peaceful, serene, quiet. Strolling among the graves, you can't help reflecting on how brief this life is, how quickly the years pass. The professor noted that Emma Goldman and "Rebel Girl" Flynn hated each other in real life (they both hated Billy Sunday) because one was a communist and the other wasn't. How ironic, he noted, that they now rest some fifteen feet from each other.

The cemetery tour may seem to disprove my point, but it doesn't. Only a handful of people came to visit a handful of the thousands of graves. With each passing day we forget a little more. If you want to be remembered after you are gone, follow the One who lives forever.

Lord of the ages, remember me. Amen.

SHINING THE LIGHT

* Name the three people who have had the greatest influence for good in your life. What quality do you remember most about each one?

* How would you like to be remembered after you are dead?

MORE LIGHT FROM GOD'S WORD
Read Psalms 9:5–6; 145:4–5; and Luke 23:42.

✳

Six

BIG GOD AND LITTLE ME

I, the Teacher, was king over Israel in Jerusalem. I devoted myself to study and to explore by wisdom all that is done under heaven. What a heavy burden God has laid on men! I have seen all the things that are done under the sun; all of them are meaningless, a chasing after the wind.

Ecclesiastes 1:12–14

Over the years I have come to understand that there are only two theologies in the world. Here they are in very simple form: There is BIG GOD and Little Me or there is Little God and BIG ME. When you come into the knowledge of God, you will have a Big God and a little you. But for most of us, it's the other way around. Our view of ourselves is so big that God shrinks down to a manageable size. But the Bible has a special name for a god you can manage. It's called an idol! Men make idols because they want a god that serves their purposes.

The God of the Bible is far bigger than we imagine. He cannot be contained in any building or statue made by human hands! The bigger your God, the smaller your view of yourself, and the quicker you will fall down in worship and praise.

Why are we here? To know God. Until you understand that, you have missed the purpose for life itself.

This is the "heavy burden" Solomon mentions in verse 13—the unending search for truth and meaning in life. God put the need to know Him inside each of us, then He made it impossible to satisfy that need with anything short of Himself. Ever since the Fall nothing in the world has worked the way it should. We live in a frustrating world, don't we? You buy something, it breaks; you fix it, it works for a while and then breaks again. Eventually it wears out completely and you have to replace it. Nothing lasts forever, nothing works right.

But it's not just creation; it's also you and me. We don't work right either. Children are born with horrible defects; people get cancer or Alzheimer's or AIDS or some other wasting disease. If you live long enough, you'll have a stroke or a heart attack or grow senile and end up in a nursing home. That's what Paul means when he says the whole creation groans waiting for its redemption (Romans 8:22). The world is broken beyond human repair, and only God can fix it.

"Give me a lever long enough," said Archimedes, "and a place to stand and I will move the world." The problem isn't the lever; it's finding a place to stand. You cannot explain the world from the standpoint of the world. The answer must come from somewhere else. Our search for truth will always lead to despair until our search leads us back to God.

If knowing God is that important, I wonder what He will have to do to get our attention. Our biggest problem is not that God isn't speaking; it's that we're so busy we can't (or won't) slow down long enough to hear His voice.

Father, my mind is filled with many questions I cannot answer. Although I do not have all the light I would desire, I certainly have all that I need. Help me to believe what I already know to be true. Amen.

— ✳ —

SHINING THE LIGHT

✳ How big is your God?

✳ In what areas of your Christian life are you struggling most right now? Do you need to slow down so you can hear God's voice?

— ✳ —

MORE LIGHT FROM GOD'S WORD

Read Job 11:7–8; Isaiah 55:8–9; and 1 Corinthians 8:1–2.

———— ✳ ————

Seven

CUT IT DOWN AND FORGET ABOUT IT

What is twisted cannot be straightened; what is lacking cannot be counted.

Ecclesiastes 1:15

Here are two stories to ponder. One comes from the Civil War, the other from the Vietnam War.

In Charles Bracelen Flood's book *Lee: The Last Years*, Flood tells of a time after the Civil War when Robert E. Lee visited a woman who took him to the remains of a grand old tree in front of her home. There she cried bitterly that its limbs and trunk had been destroyed by Union artillery fire. She waited for Lee to condemn the North or at least sympathize with her loss. Lee paused, and then said, "Cut it down, my dear madam, and then forget it."

Good advice from a man who knew the horrors of war and suffered the pain of defeat.

The second story comes from a recent interview with the newly appointed U.S. ambassador to Vietnam, Pete Peterson. Mr. Peterson's appointment was ironic because he served six years as a prisoner of war in the dreaded "Hanoi Hilton" prison camp. Now he would return to the land where he was held captive—returning not for revenge, but to represent the United States. When asked how he could do such a thing after years of starvation, torture, and inhuman brutality, he replied, "I'm not angry. I left that at the gates of the prison when I walked out in 1972. That may sound simplistic to some people, but it's the truth. I just left it behind me and decided to move forward with my life."

This week a simple thought has come to my mind more than once. It goes like this:

I can't go back.
I can't stay here.
I must go forward.

You can't go back to the past—not to relive the good times or to seek revenge for the bad times. But you can't stay where you are either. Life is like a river that flows endlessly onward. It matters not whether you are happy in your present situation or seek deliverance from it. You can't stay where you are forever. The only way to go is forward.

A man whose wife suffered greatly at the hands of her enemies told me that she had taken a "vow of silence" regarding her critics. She decided that rather than lower herself to the level of her critics, she would simply not reply at all. This is difficult, but at least it frees a person to move forward with God.

When you're tempted to get even with those who hurt you, remember that you can't go back, you can't stay where you are, but by God's grace, you can move forward one step at a time.

> *My Father, when I am tempted to live in the past, help*
> *me to remember that You are the God of new begin-*
> *nings. Amen.*

— ✳ —

SHINING THE LIGHT

✳ Is there something troubling you that you need to cut
down and forget about? What hinders you from doing that right now?

✳ Do you need to take a "vow of silence" regarding anyone in your life?

— ✳ —

MORE LIGHT FROM GOD'S WORD

Read 2 Chronicles 20:17; Philippians 3:12–14; and
2 Peter 3:18.

Eight

WHAT KNOWLEDGE CAN'T DO

I thought to myself, "Look, I have grown and increased in wisdom more than anyone who has ruled over Jerusalem before me; I have experienced much of wisdom and knowledge." Then I applied myself to the understanding of wisdom, and also of madness and folly, but I learned that this, too, is a chasing after the wind. For with much wisdom comes much sorrow; the more knowledge, the more grief.

Ecclesiastes 1:16–18

Verses 16–18 are not an argument against knowledge but a warning that knowledge isn't the answer to everything. In Jeremiah 9:23–24 the Lord Himself reminds us not to boast in our riches, strength, or wisdom, "but let him who boasts boast about this: that he understands and knows me." We were made to know God! That is our privilege, our calling, and our very purpose for existing. It is a privilege afforded to every believer and a duty every Christian must pursue.

We can always know God better than we do. No one ever arrives at a perfect knowledge of God. Those who do not know God have missed the central truth of the universe. Second Thessalonians 1 warns us that God will judge those who do not know Him. In that great day, no excuses will be accepted and no substitute knowledge will suffice. Since it is possible and necessary to know God, those who do not know Him face a terrible future.

Well-known scientist Carl Sagan died at the age of sixty-two. He gained his public fame primarily as host of the series "Cosmos" on public television. He is remembered for his oft-repeated statement that "the cosmos is all that ever was, or is, or ever will be." He was a thoroughgoing secularist, humanist, agnostic, and ardent evolutionist. To the very end he remained skeptical of any claims to God's existence. He died as he lived—an unbeliever.

After his death his wife said the following: "There was no deathbed conversion, no appeals to God, no hope for an afterlife, no pretending that he and I, who had been inseparable for twenty years, were not saying good-bye forever."

That statement reminds me of a brief anecdote J. I. Packer told regarding an acquaintance whose career derailed because of his evangelical convictions. When asked if he harbored any ill feelings, he replied quite simply: "I've known God and they haven't." Packer goes on to note most of us would not feel comfortable speaking in such straightforward terms. But the terms are entirely biblical. Knowing God does make a difference and is the defining characteristic of those who follow Jesus Christ. To know God deeply and intimately more than makes up for the things we lose because of our faith.

Lord of all the universe, save me from the folly of thinking that I know more than I really do. If I boast, let it be because I know You. Amen.

———✳———

SHINING THE LIGHT

✳ Can you think of a time when knowledge brought you sorrow?

✳ Would you feel comfortable saying, "I've known God and they haven't"?

✳ What difference does knowing God make in your life?

———✳———

MORE LIGHT FROM GOD'S WORD

Read John 17:1–3; 1 Corinthians 2:1–5; and Philippians 3:10.

✴

Nine

EAT DESSERT FIRST

I thought in my heart, "Come now, I will test you with plea-
sure to find out what is good." But that also proved to be
meaningless. "Laughter," I said, "is foolish. And what does
pleasure accomplish?" I tried cheering myself with wine, and
embracing folly—my mind still guiding me with wisdom. I
wanted to see what was worthwhile for men to do under
heaven during the few days of their lives.

Ecclesiastes 2:1–3

Solomon's search led him from wisdom to pleasure—
especially pursuit of pleasure as an end in itself. He
tried laughter, wine, and the party scene. All the while he
didn't lose his perspective but observed hedonism as a
philosophy of life. In the end he found it empty. As verse
3 makes clear, no one lives forever. In light of your on-
coming death, why not party hearty?

A certain restaurant placed the following sign in a
front window: "Life is short. Eat dessert first." Besides
being a catchy advertisement for cheesecake and apple
pie, the sign conveys a fascinating message.

Life is short. On every hand we see the evidence that
no one lives forever. The ever-changing obituary notices
remind us that one day we too will die. Or to make it
more personal, one day I will die and one day you will die.

But what insight follows from that undeniable truth? The sign suggests a thought along these lines: "Since you don't know how long you are going to live, eat dessert first because you don't want to die eating mashed potatoes." Or something like that.

I find a certain wisdom in that approach. There are some foods I prefer not to eat dead or alive—tuna fish and brussels sprouts being high on that list. So, yes, I'd prefer to have a chocolate eclair rather than a tuna casserole.

But there is another side to all this. "Eat dessert first" seems to imply that the real purpose of life is personal pleasure. But does not experience teach us to "work first, then play hard"? A menu of nothing but sweets will eventually rot your teeth and give you a very unhappy tummy. Likewise, you only appreciate your pleasure when it comes as a reward for hard work well done.

Life is short. Work hard, play hard, love God with all your heart, take each day as a blessing from the Lord, enjoy your family, love your neighbor as yourself, take time to pray and to smell the coffee. In so doing, you will find what the psalmist called the "light of life" (56:13)—and you may even discover that tuna fish can be as tasty as apple pie.

Heavenly Father, I pray for the genuine joy of the Lord to fill my life today. Amen.

— ✳ —

SHINING THE LIGHT

✳ Name three people who exhibit the joy of the Lord. What characteristics do those people have in common?

✳ What is the essential difference between happiness and joy?

— ✳ —

MORE LIGHT FROM GOD'S WORD

Read Nehemiah 8:10–18; Psalm 16:11; and Ephesians 5:18–21.

Ten

---✳---

THE MAN WHO HAD IT ALL

I undertook great projects: I built houses for myself and planted vineyards. I made gardens and parks and planted all kinds of fruit trees in them. I made reservoirs to water groves of flourishing trees. I bought male and female slaves and had other slaves who were born in my house. I also owned more herds and flocks than anyone in Jerusalem before me.

Ecclesiastes 2:4–7

If you ever travel to the Holy Land, you will no doubt see the remnants of Solomon's handiwork described in verses 4–6. Even though three thousand years have passed since Solomon reigned in Jerusalem, remains of his vast building projects dot the landscape. Archeologists have uncovered his stables, numerous cities he fortified, and underneath the Temple Mount in Jerusalem they have excavated the enormous stones that served as the foundation of the Temple itself.

He spent seven years building the Temple (1 Kings 5–6) and thirteen building his palace (1 Kings 7). First Kings 9:17–19 adds these details: "And Solomon rebuilt Gezer. He built up Lower Beth Horon, Baalath, and Tadmor in the desert, within his land, as well as all his store cities and the towns for his chariots and for his horses—

whatever he desired to build in Jerusalem, in Lebanon and throughout all the territory he ruled." First Kings 10 tells us about his throne of ivory overlaid with gold; his ships that sailed to distant ports, returning with precious metals, apes and baboons; and how silver was as plentiful as stones in Jerusalem. The whole world sought audience with the king to hear the wisdom God had put on his heart. There never was a man like Solomon—not before or since. No king ever had so many earthly advantages.

Yet the end of the story is not a happy one. Solomon's many foreign wives turned his heart away from following God fully (1 Kings 11:1–6). Unlike his father David, he was not a man after God's own heart. David was an adulterer and a murderer, but deep inside he truly wanted to please God. Solomon, for all his greatness, had character flaws that eventually caused his kingdom to split in two. He also brought idol worship into the land. That curse would not be removed for hundreds of years.

The lesson in all this is not hard to find. Wisdom alone is not enough. Solomon had more wisdom than David, but three thousand years later the world now acclaims father as greater than his son. David had many flaws, but in the end he had a heart to know God. Solomon had it all from an earthly point of view, but in the end what he had didn't matter because he didn't have the one thing that mattered most. Solomon's wisdom led him to greatness but it couldn't prevent him from sowing the seeds of his own decline. Having it all doesn't matter if the Lord is not first in your heart.

Father, I pray for a heart fully devoted to You. Amen.

———✳———

SHINING THE LIGHT

✳ What are the "great projects" of your life right now?

✳ Have you ever dedicated your efforts to the Lord Jesus Christ and asked for His blessing? Take a few moments to do that before reading any further.

———✳———

MORE LIGHT FROM GOD'S WORD

Read 1 Kings 6:1–38; 1 Corinthians 6:19–20; and Revelation 21:22.

---

*

Eleven

MONEY, SEX, AND POWER

I amassed silver and gold for myself, and the treasure of kings and provinces. I acquired men and women singers, and a harem as well—the delights of the heart of man.

Ecclesiastes 2:8

Solomon had a harem, all right—seven hundred wives and three hundred concubines. Historians tell us that many of his wives were not romantic attachments but rather convenience marriages made to cement certain foreign relationships and guarantee peaceful relations with other nations. Nevertheless, common though this practice may have been, it got Solomon in trouble and helped pave the way for the breakup of his kingdom.

I love the phrase "the delights of the heart of man." What a nice way to put it. If we say "sexual temptation" it sounds much different. Not too many years ago we went through a period in which several of America's best-known preachers fell prey to sexual sin. In each case good men who apparently loved the Lord yielded in a moment of weakness.

I am thinking now of one man I used to watch on television as he preached with great power to thousands of people. I felt then that the power of the Holy Spirit was truly upon his life. Although his behavior shocked and saddened me, I did not believe he was a religious charlatan.

But something somewhere, somehow, at some point, went tragically wrong. Did he become so big that he thought he could get away with anything? Did the empire he built finally destroy him? Did he think that he was above God's moral law? If so, he would not be the first man to fall at the height of his own power.

His downfall came when he refused to accept the discipline imposed by his own denomination. Like so many before him, he thought he could solve his problems on his own. Like so many others, he discovered too late that he couldn't do it by himself.

Years ago a friend told me, "The first price you pay is always the cheapest." Which being interpreted means, the quicker you deal with your problems, the better off you will be. We avoid facing our own moral weakness because we hope the problems will go away on their own. That almost never happens, especially in the realm of sexual sin. The price never goes down; it always goes up.

The way of transgressors is always hard, but as so many others have discovered, you don't have to make it harder by refusing the help of people who truly love you.

Loving Lord, when I am tempted to depart from Your ways, show me in advance the dangers of disobedience. Amen.

— ✳ —

SHINING THE LIGHT

* Do you agree that "the first price you pay is always the cheapest"? If so, how have you experienced this truth in your own life?

* What happens when we disregard God's teaching regarding sexual purity?

— ✳ —

MORE LIGHT FROM GOD'S WORD

Read Ezra 9:1–10:4; Proverbs 5:15–19; and Hebrews 13:4.

✳

Twelve

THE VIEW FROM THE PENTHOUSE

I became greater by far than anyone in Jerusalem before me. In all this my wisdom stayed with me.

Ecclesiastes 2:9

Here is his story, briefly told: At age six, his mother threw his birthday cake off the porch. He played the French Horn at age twelve and by the time he was fifteen he was playing professionally with some of the top jazz musicians of the day. Eventually, he became the first black musician to break the Hollywood color barrier as a composer of scores. He is perhaps best known as the composer of the score for *The Color Purple*.

But it hasn't come easy. Quincy Jones has been married three times, survived two brain surgeries, and endured a complete emotional breakdown. Several years ago he faced surgery for an aneurysm that threatened to kill him. The doctors told him that his chances of recovery were 100 to 1. Miraculously, he survived.

Question: "What did you start doing different after your operation?"

Answer: "The first thing I started doing was hugging a lot.

"When you get to be fifty, you start dealing with the countdown, and you can deal with it in a positive way or a negative way. I try to deal with it in a positive way. . . . You try to make this little life to be this great gift." Then he added these words: "You know that old cliché about your life passing in front of you? Well, it really does."

I don't know much else about Quincy Jones, but his philosophy of life makes sense to me. What do you do when the doctors tell you that there is virtually no chance you will survive the operation, and then you open your eyes and you find out you aren't dead after all? You were the 1 in 100 who made it.

You take a good look at life and then you start hugging a lot. It makes you take stock of the passing days and you realize that you cheated the Grim Reaper, but only temporarily. Suddenly life takes on a new meaning. You see it as it really is, as the most precious gift you will ever possess, a gift that must someday be returned to the Giver.

If you are smart, you start hugging a lot, because when you get down to it, the relationships you have with the people you love matter more than the awards and the roar of the crowd. That's just fluff and frosting and window dressing.

The only tragedy is that too often it takes a tragedy to make us wake up and figure out what's really important in life.

Lord Jesus, thank You for using the hard times of life to rearrange my priorities. Amen.

— ✳ —

SHINING THE LIGHT

✳ Who is the wealthiest person you know? As far as you know, where does this person stand with the Lord?

✳ What is the major temptation a rich person faces with regard to his own wealth?

— ✳ —

MORE LIGHT FROM GOD'S WORD

Read 1 Corinthians 1:26–31; Colossians 2:2–3; and James 3:13–18.

Thirteen

---------- ✳ ----------

KING FOR A DAY

I denied myself nothing my eyes desired; I refused my heart no pleasure. My heart took delight in all my work, and this was the reward for all my labor.

Ecclesiastes 2:10

Have you ever wondered what it would be like to be king for a day? Suppose that for just one day you had unlimited wealth, unlimited power, and could do anything you wanted. You could ask for a jet and fly anywhere in the world. Or you could go on a shopping spree in Beverly Hills and never run out of money. Or you could buy a new home—or two or three—and still have enough to buy one hundred homes tomorrow.

Solomon had all that—and not just for one day but every day. If he saw it, he bought it. If he wanted it, he took it. If he thought he would enjoy it, he tried it. His investigation of the pleasures of life took him in every direction and brought him great delight. Put simply: He enjoyed being the king and the richest man on earth.

This leads to an interesting observation. Some people can be rich in the will of God. I think that God sometimes blesses men and women with an abundance of wealth as a kind of test. While poverty certainly poses its own set of problems, so does wealth. The apostle Paul reminds us that "*the love of money* is a root of all kinds of evil" (1 Timothy 6:10, italics added). Money itself is morally neutral. The same dollar that buys pornography may also be used to support a missionary in Thailand. It can fuel greed or it can feed a hungry child. Money has no moral value except as we use it for good or for evil. Since that is true, it follows that every dime we spend represents a moral choice.

Christianity is a giving religion. It starts with God who gave His Son—the "indescribable gift" of 2 Corinthians 9:15. It is "indescribable" because of its extent. For if I were to go to the bank and withdraw all my money and give it away, and if I were to sell my car and give the money to the poor, and if I were to give everything I had and then gave myself as someone's slave . . . I wouldn't have given as much as God did when He gave His only begotten Son.

God can never owe me anything. I can never outgive Him. When I come to the end of my philanthropy and begin to pat myself on the back for being such a wonderful person, God bids me to look to the Cross and see the bleeding Son of God. Then I realize I know nothing of what real giving is.

Spirit of God, I thank You that I have all that I need and more besides. Help me to become a generous giver. Amen.

— ✳ —

SHINING THE LIGHT

* If you had Solomon's power, what pleasure would you choose for yourself today?

* The Westminster Confession says that man was created to glorify God and enjoy Him forever. What does "enjoying God forever" mean to you? What keeps you from enjoying God more than you do?

— ✳ —

MORE LIGHT FROM GOD'S WORD

Read Genesis 1:31; Psalm 63:1–5; and 1 Timothy 4:4.

✴

Fourteen

SO WHAT?

Yet when I surveyed all that my hands had done and what I had toiled to achieve, everything was meaningless, a chasing after the wind; nothing was gained under the sun.

Ecclesiastes 2:11

You would think Solomon would be happy. After all, he had it all—money, fame, power, a vast harem, an enormous kingdom, ships that brought him riches from foreign shores, a nation at peace, the respect and admiration of his fellow monarchs, a temple that was the wonder of his day, and the affection of a grateful nation. Really, what more could a man ask for?

Good question. Evidently whatever he lacked wasn't in the material realm, because he quite simply had reached the top of the heap. There weren't any other mountains to climb. It is reminiscent of Alexander the Great who died at age thirty-three having conquered the known world.

What had Solomon gained? In the end, nothing. It was all vanity, emptiness, and chasing after the wind. And that brought him back to God—which is where all of Solomon's journeys eventually ended up.

We often say, "Jesus is all I need." But you will never know if Jesus is all you need until Jesus is all you have.

When Jesus is all you have, then you discover that Jesus is all you need.

The more I think about that, the more profound it seems to me. For most of us, "Jesus is all I need" is little more than a Christian cliché—a bumper sticker slogan and nothing more. But recently I visited a friend who is dying of cancer. There is no hope for her recovery—a fact that is completely clear in her mind. With a wry smile she said, "Jesus has been so good to me. If He wants to take me home now, I'm ready to go. Whatever the Lord wants is all right with me."

Where does that kind of faith come from?

Ask the single moms; they know all about it. Ask the man who just lost his job; he knows about it. Ask the woman who is struggling with the shattering pain of divorce—she has learned the truth over and over again. Ask that young girl whose father died when she was fifteen. Or the man whose wife has Alzheimer's disease. Or the young couple who lost their first child.

Gordon MacDonald said, "I have discovered that your theology is only as deep as your pain." Pity those who have an easy life. They never really know Jesus.

If pain has any advantage, it is this: When we hurt, we find out if what we believe is really true. Many can testify through their tears: "When everything else was gone, I turned to Jesus and He was still there."

Is Jesus all you need? Yes, but you'll never know for sure until Jesus is all you have. And when Jesus is all you have, to your utter surprise you'll discover that everything you always heard is true—Jesus is all you need.

Lord of my life, may I never expect to find lasting happiness in the world, but only in You. Amen.

—✳—

SHINING THE LIGHT

✳ Why wasn't Solomon happy? Would you have been happy?

✳ How has God used pain to deepen your walk with Him?

—✳—

MORE LIGHT FROM GOD'S WORD

Read Genesis 32:22–26; Proverbs 15:16–17; and Luke 18:18–30.

---
*

Fifteen

THE TURTLE ON
THE FENCE POST

*Then I turned my thoughts to consider wisdom, and also
madness and folly. What more can the king's successor do
than what has already been done?*

Ecclesiastes 2:12

I'm sure Solomon felt pressure from both sides on the
issue of kingly succession. On the one hand his father
was David, who quite frankly was a better man than he
would ever be—even though Solomon was technically a
greater king. Matthew 1:1 called the Lord Jesus Christ
the "son of David," not the "son of Solomon," though
that title is also correct. Solomon lived and reigned in the
shadow of his father, and I am sure he knew that no matter what he did, he could never eclipse his father's place in
the hearts of his people.

Then there was the matter of his successor. Transfer-
ring power is always a tricky business, but Solomon didn't
help himself by all the foreign wives he married and the
consequent introduction of idolatry into Israel. First
Kings 11 plainly says that God used the rebellion of Jer-
oboam to wrest the kingdom from Solomon's hands in
judgment for Solomon's sins in the latter years of his
reign. Solomon evidently knew nothing about God's de-

cision. He died thinking that Rehoboam his son would rule the whole nation as he had done. However, his son proved to be too proud to listen to wise counsel and levied a severe tax on the people. The northern ten tribes revolted. That left the tribes of Benjamin and Judah—a tiny remnant of Solomon's vast empire.

In the end Solomon was not as great as his father but much greater than his son. His reign would be remembered as Israel's Golden Age—a time when the borders of the nation reached their zenith. With much pride Solomon asked in Ecclesiastes 2:12: "What more can the king's successor do than what has already been done?" But Solomon was wrong. He could not outstrip King David as a military leader or as a poet.

Perhaps the lesson here has something to do with the dangers of pride. It is no surprise that the ancient church fathers listed pride as the first of the Seven Deadly Sins. First because it destroys more people than any other sin; because it comes in unawares and does so much damage; and also because religious people are so susceptible. Pride, remember, was the sin that caused Satan to fall from heaven.

In his office, noted author Alex Haley had a painting of a turtle on top of a fence post. When people asked him why he had the painting, he replied that it reminded him of a great truth: Whenever you see a turtle on a fence post, you know he didn't get there by himself. Somebody had to put him there.

The next time you are feeling a little puffed up about

all the great things you have done, and you are about to break your arm patting yourself on the back, remember the turtle on the fence post. You didn't crawl to the top by yourself. Somebody had to put you there.

Eternal Father, help me live so that those who come after me won't be ashamed to follow in my steps. Amen.

— ✳ —

SHINING THE LIGHT

✳ Why is it often difficult to follow a successful person?

✳ Whose steps are you following? And who is following you right now?

— ✳ —

MORE LIGHT FROM GOD'S WORD
Read Joshua 1:1–3; Malachi 3:7; and Hebrews 11:17.

Sixteen

AM I WISE OR AM
I FOOLISH?

I saw that wisdom is better than folly, just as light is better than darkness. The wise man has eyes in his head, while the fool walks in the darkness; but I came to realize that the same fate overtakes them both.

Ecclesiastes 2:13–14

Sergei Nikolaev, pastor of the Temple of the Gospel in St. Petersburg, Russia, knows Billy Graham well, having served as the evangelist's translator during one of Graham's missions to Moscow. Somehow the question came up: Why is Billy Graham so effective? Pastor Nikolaev said that in his opinion Billy Graham's sermons are not profound. They are usually incredibly simple, so simple that learned scholars dismiss him because he doesn't use high-sounding language or speak with theological subtlety.

What is the evangelist's secret? "It is the way he presents his message," Pastor Nikolaev answered. "When you listen to Billy Graham, he preaches it in such a way that you can only come to one conclusion: If I am a normal person, I must say yes to Jesus Christ." Dr. Graham preaches so that the only logical, rational decision is to come to Christ. Therefore, Pastor Nikolaev said, the hearer must ask himself this question: Am I normal or am I crazy? If I am normal, I must accept Christ. So Dr. Graham is constantly bringing people to ask the question: Am I smart or am I stupid? Am I wise or am I foolish?

During one Graham crusade in St. Petersburg, a very brilliant architect, an atheist, came to hear him. Night after night he listened to the preaching of the gospel. He didn't make a decision during the crusade. As he thought about the matter later, he realized the question was not "What should I do with Jesus?" but rather "Am I smart or am I stupid?" And so while he was taking a shower one day, it all came together for him. With the water splashing in his face, he looked to heaven and said, "Jesus Christ, forgive my sins." In that moment, he was saved, and his sins were forgiven. He is now active in Pastor Nikolaev's church.

So I ask: Are you wise or are you foolish?

Remember, you can't help being a sinner. That comes by virtue of being a descendant of Adam. But God has made a way for you to pass from Adam to Christ. Your first birth put you in Adam; your second birth puts you in Christ. That's why Jesus said, "You must be born again."

Have you ever been born again? Have you ever passed from death to life? If you are in Adam, don't despair. You don't have to stay there. You can come to Christ right now. It's the smartest move you'll ever make.

Lord Jesus, I am trusting You and You alone as my only hope for eternal salvation. Amen.

———✳———

SHINING THE LIGHT

✳ Do you believe that trusting Christ is the wisest decision any person can make? Why or why not?

✳ Are your sins forgiven?

———✳———

MORE LIGHT FROM GOD'S WORD

Read Proverbs 4:18–19; John 16:8; and Romans 1:21–22.

Seventeen

TEMPORARY ADVANTAGES

Then I thought in my heart, "The fate of the fool will over-
take me also. What then do I gain by being wise?" I said in
my heart, "This too is meaningless." For the wise man, like
the fool, will not be long remembered; in days to come both
will be forgotten. Like the fool, the wise man too must die!

Ecclesiastes 2:15–16

Some years ago an artist painted a picture showing a mountain of skulls. At first glance all the skulls seem to be the same, but when the observer looked closely he noticed some writing on each skull. One said "doctor," another "teacher," another "secretary," another "technician," another "salesman"; still others were labeled "foreman," "driver," "captain," "lawyer," and "judge." There were hundreds of skulls in the painting, each one representing a different occupation.

The artist and Solomon would agree. No matter what your position in this life may be, you will eventually die. Rich man, poor man, beggar man, thief—they all die sooner or later. In one sense, this is certainly true. You will eventually die. No one escapes death forever, no matter how much one may try or how hard he exercises or how carefully he avoids catastrophe. The Grim Reaper knocks on every door sooner or later.

Yet there is another side to the truth. While death comes eventually to all men, death does not erase all the distinctions between men. From the standpoint of the Christian faith, it is at death that the real differences among people become apparent. I speak not of the artificial differences of money, power, fame, and worldly achievement. Those truly will all perish with the grave.

Years ago I received a phone call at 10:30 P.M. Someone had died. Would I please call the family? Before I could pick up the phone a second time, the mother called me. Her son had taken drugs and had died earlier that evening. As I got dressed to go to the home, I wondered what I would say. When I got there everyone was milling around in a state of confusion. At length the mother took me aside and through her tears she asked me the inevitable question, the question I had known was coming: "Why? Why did God let this happen to my son?"

As I recall, the young man had been a bouncer at a topless nightclub. At the funeral, I preached the gospel to row upon row of rough-looking people who seemed frightened to be in the same room with their dead friend. Afterwards the reception area was blue with cigarette smoke as if everyone lit up at the same time to calm their collective nerves.

But then I think of many other funerals I have done across the years. Without fail, whenever the time comes to bury a Christian, along with the sorrow comes an enormous amount of joy. There is triumph as the people of God rehearse the promise of God—of resurrection to life in heaven—even as they lay their loved ones to rest.

What happens when you die depends on what happens to you before you die. Jesus Christ makes the difference.

Lord Jesus, You showed us how to live and You showed us how to die. I want to follow in Your steps so that I'll be ready when my time comes. Amen.

— ✳ —

SHINING THE LIGHT

✳ How does the Christian gospel answer the problem of death?

✳ Why is the life Jesus offers truly "eternal" life? Have you received the gift of eternal life through faith in Christ?

— ✳ —

MORE LIGHT FROM GOD'S WORD
Read Psalm 49:10–11; 2 Timothy 1:10; and 1 John 5:12.

✳

Eighteen

"I HATED LIFE"

So I hated life, because the work that is done under the sun was grievous to me. All of it is meaningless, a chasing after the wind.

Ecclesiastes 2:17

Sometimes I get so lonely it's unbelievable. Life has been so good to me. I've got a great wife, good kids, money, my own health—and I'm lonely and bored. . . . I often wondered why so many rich people commit suicide. Money sure isn't a cure-all." Those were the words of O. J. Simpson in 1978.

More people than we know have said with Solomon, "I hated life." Not all of them have thought about suicide, but many have and more than we'll ever know have taken at least one step in that direction.

What happens to those who commit suicide? Does God automatically send them to hell? I believe the answer is no. Romans 8:38–39 contains Paul's triumphant statement that nothing can separate us from the love of God in Christ Jesus our Lord. He lists a succession of extreme opposites: height or depth, length or breadth, things present or things to come. He includes "neither death nor life." By life he means all the various experiences of life: No matter how difficult our circumstances, how discouraging our defeats, how frustrating our days may be, how badly others may mistreat us—nothing in this life can separate us from the love of God.

It's true. You may lose your wealth, your health, your happiness, your friends, your influence, your job, and everything you have worked for. But no one can take Jesus away from you. You are saved and saved forever. God's love is secure despite the discouragements of life.

But note that the apostle writes "neither death nor life." That can only mean one thing. Death itself cannot conquer the child of God. The grave has lost its victory; death has lost its sting.

Death separates us from many things—from our loved ones, from our friends, from our conscious life on this earth, from all that we have said and done and accomplished—all of that vanishes when we die, but death cannot win the one battle that matters. It cannot separate us from the love of God in Christ Jesus.

But what about suicide? Surely you don't believe that suicide is stronger than God's love. A man or a woman may, in a desperate, sad moment feel so trapped, so oppressed, so discouraged, so angry, so despondent that they may take their own life. Can that act, you wonder, separate us from the love of God? No.

Do some people who commit suicide go to hell? Yes, but not because of the death they died, but because of the life they lived. Suicide doesn't send people to hell. Sin sends people to hell, especially the greatest sin, the sin of saying "No" to Jesus Christ.

The real issue of life and death is this: What have you done with Jesus Christ? The issue isn't suicide; it's Jesus Christ. What have you done with Him? That's the one decision that determines where you go when you die.

Lord, may I not count my life so important that I forget to look beyond it to eternity. Give me eyes to see what lies beyond the river. Amen.

———✳———

SHINING THE LIGHT

* Have you ever felt like saying, "I hate my life"? If so, what did you do about it?

* How do you handle times of discouragement in your own life?

———✳———

MORE LIGHT FROM GOD'S WORD

Read Luke 14:26; John 10:10; and Revelation 12:11.

***

Nineteen

PASSING THE BATON

I hated all the things I had toiled for under the sun, because I must leave them to the one who comes after me. And who knows whether he will be a wise man or a fool? Yet he will have control over all the work into which I have poured my effort and skill under the sun. This too is meaningless.

Ecclesiastes 2:18–19

It turns out that Solomon was quite right to worry about his successor. His son Rehoboam was so inept as a leader that he presided over the breakup of the kingdom. Perhaps Solomon saw some character defect in his son and feared the worst. In the early chapters of Proverbs he appeals over and over to "my son" to heed his words, turn from wickedness, and seek wisdom with all his heart. Check out these verses: Proverbs 1:10; 2:1; 3:1; 3:11; 4:20; 5:1; 5:20; and 6:20. These are only a few of the verses where Solomon appeals to his son's heart. From our vantage point we perhaps tend to read those verses in a generic sense—as if Solomon is writing for young people in general. But perhaps there is something deeper here—the anxious heart of a father who knows that one day he will have to hand over to his son all that he has spent a lifetime building.

I know of no way to guarantee that your children will

follow in your steps. Children have minds of their own, and in the end our sons and daughters must choose for themselves whether they will serve the Lord. However, I do believe we can tip the scales in the right direction by the way we live day to day. Training up a child in the way he should go (Proverbs 22:6) certainly means living a consistent Christian life. Our kids have excellent baloney detectors and can smell a phony a mile away. On the other hand, we don't have to be perfect either. Consistency matters, time spent with our children matters, prayer matters, and faith matters.

Children make many mistakes in the course of life, but those raised in godly homes will be inclined toward righteousness. Christian parents need to take the long view when evaluating how their children are doing. Many teenagers and young adults go through a period of questioning values and testing their limits. But the good seed planted in childhood will eventually bear fruit, though not necessarily as soon as we would like or as abundantly as we would like.

Our children belong to the Lord, not to us. This is a hard lesson to learn, and most of us have to relearn it many times. They are gifts from the Lord, entrusted to our care for a few brief years.

A few months ago I heard someone say a most reassuring thing: "God is not worried about your children." He knows them better than we do and He loves them with an everlasting love. He will not stop until His work in them is complete. Our part is to be faithful, and God will take care of the rest.

Help me to pass along my faith, O Lord, so that the things I believe in won't die with me. Amen.

— ✳ —

SHINING THE LIGHT

✳ What steps have you taken to prepare for the distribution of your assets after you die? What steps do you still need to take?

✳ What can you do to pass along your faith to those who will come after you?

— ✳ —

MORE LIGHT FROM GOD'S WORD

Read Genesis 47:29–30; 50:24–25; Joshua 24:32; and Hebrews 11:22.

Twenty

✳

GOD'S CURE FOR
ANXIOUS CARE

*So my heart began to despair over all my toilsome labor un-
der the sun. For a man may do his work with wisdom,
knowledge and skill, and then he must leave all he owns to
someone who has not worked for it. This too is meaningless
and a great misfortune. What does a man get for all the toil
and anxious striving with which he labors under the sun?
All his days his work is pain and grief; even at night his
mind does not rest. This too is meaningless.*

Ecclesiastes 2:20–23

The king sounds a little depressed in the above verses,
doesn't he? I can't blame him for his down-to-earth
honesty. Nothing numbs the heart more than realizing
that your children don't appreciate what you have done
for them. As Ecclesiastes makes clear, there are no guarantees in this life—except that one day we will die. Everything is up for grabs.

The foundation of gratitude is the expectation of
nothing. Often we live in disappointment because we expect more than life has to offer. Many of us complain
about the thorns when we ought to give thanks for the
roses. If we expected less, we would be more grateful. We
complain because we think we deserve more than we

have. The less you expect out of life, the more you can be grateful for every blessing you receive.

In the end we all receive far more than we deserve. The Christian gospel teaches us that God gives us what we don't deserve (salvation) and withholds from us what we do deserve (punishment). Somehow we accept this truth when it comes to salvation but neatly overlook it when we evaluate our lives on a daily basis.

Some friends moved to Ireland to begin a new ministry. It hasn't been an easy transition. In a letter the wife wrote without regret of what she is missing—especially her two-year-old nephew's birthday party. Her heart longs to be with her extended family, but she has no doubts about the path she and her husband have chosen. "There is the calm assurance that this is where we're supposed to be (most days, that is)." I appreciate the parenthetical comment and the little smiley-face she drew beside it. That makes it very real.

Is it worth it? she wonders. Then she ponders what Jesus said about losing your life for His sake and gaining it in the end. Here is her conclusion: "That compels me to recognize the joy I have in living where He wants me—even on the days when I don't feel happy to be here." How wonderful that statement is. Because she is where God wants her, she can have joy even when she isn't particularly happy to be there.

If you know that God is sovereign, then you can be content—and even find joy—in the midst of circumstances that are less than ideal.

Lord, I do not pray for a lighter load but I do ask for stronger shoulders. Amen.

— ✳ —

SHINING THE LIGHT

✳ Are you a worrier? How would your friends answer that question?

✳ Stop and pray about your three greatest concerns at this moment.

— ✳ —

MORE LIGHT FROM GOD'S WORD

Read Psalm 119:165; Isaiah 26:3; and Philippians 4:4–7.

Twenty-One

LEARNING TO ENJOY LIFE

A man can do nothing better than to eat and drink and find satisfaction in his work. This too, I see, is from the hand of God, for without him, who can eat or find enjoyment?

Ecclesiastes 2:24–25

Twice in verses 24–25 Solomon speaks of "finding" satisfaction and "finding" enjoyment. He then informs us that while we are called to search, we will never find what we are looking for unless God gives it to us. This calls to mind the staccato commands of the apostle Paul: "Rejoice always; pray without ceasing; in everything give thanks" (1 Thessalonians 5:16–18 NASB). Someone has called these three commands "the standing orders of the gospel." They are "standing orders" because they always apply to every Christian in every situation.

This is a great challenge, isn't it? After all, we would have no problem if the text said: "Rejoice sometimes"; "Pray occasionally"; and "Give thanks when you feel like it."

That's the way most of us live—on the "sometimes, occasionally, when you feel like it" plane of life. How do we rise to the higher level of "always," "without ceasing," and "everything"? Surely it relates to how we view the goodness of God.

I know one family living in a very difficult and some-times dangerous area of the world. Yet the parents believe this is where God wants them to be. After recounting many of the setbacks and heartaches that are routine to missionary work, they included this telling paragraph. As much as anything else, it explains how a person can rise to the level of giving thanks in every situation:

Believers in our country frequently have a "Thanks-giving" offering, or even a special service. These offerings are usually given by grateful members of the congrega-tion—even after a tragic event. Yes, in ALL things we are to give God our thanksgiving and gratitude. It is in-teresting that one of the standard greeting lines here is: Q: "How is the work?" A: "We thank God."

I do not mean to suggest that this is easy, only that it is absolutely necessary. As hard as it may be to rejoice al-ways, what is your alternative? To give in to despair and anger? If you refuse to give thanks in every situation, you are virtually saying that you know better than God how to run the universe. By giving thanks when we don't feel like it, we are proclaiming that God's wisdom is greater than ours. That simple act of giving thanks in the midst of sorrow and heartache is a testimony worth more than 10,000 words spoken when things are going well. Per-haps we should end this section with a prayer by George Herbert:

Gracious God, You have given so much to me. Give me one thing more—a grateful heart. Amen.

— ✳ —

SHINING THE LIGHT

✳ How much joy does God give you?

✳ Have you ever thanked God for the prayers He didn't answer? Take a moment and ask God for the gift of a grateful heart.

— ✳ —

MORE LIGHT FROM GOD'S WORD

Read Nehemiah 12:31–42; Psalm 103; and Revelation 4:9–11.

✳

Twenty-Two

ARE YOU ON GOD'S SIDE?

To the man who pleases him, God gives wisdom, knowledge and happiness, but to the sinner he gives the task of gathering and storing up wealth to hand it over to the one who pleases God. This too is meaningless, a chasing after the wind.

Ecclesiastes 2:26

Verse 26 reminds us that there is a moral government in the universe. God honors those who honor Him (1 Samuel 2:30), and He judges those who sin against Him. The casual reader may skip right over the particular judgment Solomon has in mind. He suggests that the wicked store up wealth to give it to the righteous. This is a startling thought. It implies a number of interesting ideas, including the idea that sinners are just as much under God's ultimate control as the righteous. When we sing "He's got the whole world in His hands," we don't usually think about sinners being in His hands, but they are.

Beyond that, we may also say that God orders events so that the righteous will often profit from the work of sinners. Proverbs 13:22 states the same truth in a different context: "A good man leaves an inheritance for his children's children, but a sinner's wealth is stored up for the righteous." And Proverbs 28:8 offers a similar statement: "He who increases his wealth by exorbitant interest amasses it for another, who will be kind to the poor." Matthew Henry suggests that God "tantalizes" sinners by giving them wealth only to take it away later and give it to the righteous. God does it by an "overruling providence" so that the ungodly are compelled to yield their riches to the children of God. He offers as an example how the Canaanites kept the good land until God gave it to the children of Israel. We might also think of Mordecai receiving the king's signet ring after the death of Haman (Esther 8:2). Mordecai ends up receiving the estate of wicked Haman, who plotted against the Lord's people.

Several questions might be asked at this point, chief among them being, Why doesn't this happen all the time? The basic answer is we do not know; but I confess that I find much comfort in the words of Martin Luther King, Jr.: "The arm of the universe is long but it bends toward justice."

We will never understand the inequities of life when we take a short-term view. Bad things do happen to good people and bad people sometimes get away with murder. One man gets cancer and dies at forty-two; another lives for ninety-five years—but the first man was godly and the second was not. How can this be? The person of faith must assume that there are other factors that go beyond what we can see.

However, if we take the long-term view our vision becomes much clearer. There truly is a moral order to the universe. God does honor those who honor Him. He judges sinners and rewards the righteous. The reward often comes in this life, but if not God has an eternity to set right what has gone wrong. In the end no one will ever regret serving the Lord.

Lord, I do not ask that You be on my side, only that I be on Yours. Amen.

SHINING THE LIGHT

* What three adjectives would you use to describe the life that pleases God?

* Do you believe it pays to serve God? Name some ways God rewards His children in this life.

———✳———

MORE LIGHT FROM GOD'S WORD

Read 2 Chronicles 30:20–21; Hosea 14:9; and Romans 2:6–11.

※

Twenty-Three

EACH PRECIOUS MOMENT

There is a time for everything, and a season for every activity under heaven.

Ecclesiastes 3:1

Missionary friends in Nigeria have told me that Africans and Americans hold radically different views of time. For Westerners, time is to be managed, obeyed, and strictly observed. We spend large amounts of time planning for the future. We set deadlines and evaluate our performance by our ability to meet those deadlines. We start every meeting with an agenda and rarely exceed the allotted time limit.

The Nigerian generally approaches the concept of time differently. Relationships take precedence over sticking to time limits. Therefore, if a visitor drops in, the Nigerian host stops whatever he is doing to entertain his company for an appropriate amount of time, according to the relationship. If you live in Nigeria and the visitor decides to stay with you, you do not ask him or her how long the visit will last; that will reveal itself when it is important. To ask is considered rude. If spending time with this unannounced visitor makes you late for another engagement, that is OK. People generally accept that going late to any public function is normal—but one is not to leave early, which is a sign of rudeness. Meetings last until the work is done—with or without an agenda. The more important an item is, the longer there has to be discussion, even if there is already consensus. If there is not consensus, the group will continue to discuss the issue.

Another striking difference with respect to time deals with the concept of the future. Nigerian Christians speak in a way that frequently calls to mind the truth that God is in control of the number of our days. They frequently thank God for "seeing yet another day." There is also frequent reference to Christ's second coming. For example, a church announcement might sound like this: "Next Sunday evening, at 5 P.M. if the Lord tarries, the Couples' Fellowship will have a special program. All are expected to be in attendance." While those words can become routine, they also embody a biblical worldview—living with a sense of anticipation for the return of our Lord.

For all of us, time is flying. Sometimes we are so intensely looking to the future that the present rushes past unnoticed. Our challenge is to count each day as precious—knowing that what we do counts for eternity.

Almighty God, help me not to fritter away my days but to use each moment for the greatest possible good. Amen.

——✳——

SHINING THE LIGHT

* How many hours have you wasted in the last week?

* Suppose that tomorrow you were given five extra hours. How would you use them for the greatest possible good?

——*——

MORE LIGHT FROM GOD'S WORD
Read Psalm 31:15; Acts 1:7; and Romans 12:9–12.

Twenty-Four

❋

TIMES AND SEASONS

A time to be born and a time to die, a time to plant and a time to uproot, a time to kill and a time to heal, a time to tear down and a time to build.

Ecclesiastes 3:2–3

The meaning of the above verses is transparent: In this changing world, nothing stays the same. We move from one thing to another: from joy to sorrow, from war to peace and back to war again. We search for a while, then we give up. We are silent, then we speak; then we are silent again. We love and we hate—and we do it over and over again. We are born, we grow up, we give birth; our children grow up, they give birth. We die, our children die, and our grandchildren grow up and give birth.

That's what life is all about. It is part of God's plan. Some of these things we do ourselves and some are sent to us by God Himself. But they all fit into His plan. No one scatters stones all the time and no one gathers all the time (see verse 5).

Consider how this applies to the marriage relationship. If you stay married long enough, you will see it all. Everything that can happen will happen. Any couple married more than twenty years can testify to this fact. There is indescribable joy and the deepest sorrow. There is hatred and there is love. There is birth and there is death. There is success and there is failure—often back-to-back. All these things have their place and if you stay together long enough, you will see them all.

I remembered this truth when I attended the wake for a dear friend who died of cancer. About fifty people were in the room when I arrived. As I walked to the casket to pay my respects, I passed several good friends who were chatting together. There she was—resting in the casket—and not five feet away the young people were talking about cars and sports and their jobs and smiling to each other. Life and death were eerily juxtaposed against each other.

Were the others being disrespectful? No, they loved my friend as much as I did. But life goes on. Even in the midst of sorrow, those who remain speak of life. Later that evening a young couple came by with a baby barely two weeks old. There it was, plain as day, right in front of my eyes, life and death in the same room. Joy and sorrow. Hope and sadness. Yesterday and tomorrow all mixed together, all happening at once. Someone dies and we weep. Another person is born and we rejoice.

That's what Solomon was talking about. In this ever-changing world, God alone can give meaning to life; He alone does not change. He directs the jumbled events that seem to have no rhyme or reason. So cling to this truth: God is in charge and does not change, and He makes no mistakes.

My God, You are the Lord of the changing seasons of life. Without You I could hardly face tomorrow; but as long as You are with me I will have no fear. Amen.

——*——

SHINING THE LIGHT

* What "season" of life are you in right now? If you are married, how have you experienced the ups and downs of life?

* Name a circumstance in which you have seen God's faithfulness in an unexpected way.

——*——

MORE LIGHT FROM GOD'S WORD

Read Ezekiel 18:30–32; 1 Peter 4:1–5; and Revelation 1:17–18.

✳

Twenty-Five

A TIME TO LAUGH ...

A time to weep and a time to laugh, a time to mourn and a time to dance, a time to scatter stones and a time to gather them, a time to embrace and a time to refrain.

Ecclesiastes 3:4–5

Several years ago I traveled to Russia on a speaking tour of evangelical churches. Although I don't speak much Russian, it was easy to communicate because the Russian people are by nature warm and friendly. I found two things true of every Russian Christian I met: They love to sing and they love to laugh. Everywhere I went, from St. Petersburg to the Volga River, we sang together, traded stories, and told jokes. They laughed at my fractured Russian (delivered with a Southern accent), and I laughed at their stories, even when I didn't understand (which was most of the time).

My travels through Russia taught me that laughter is the universal language. If you have a sense of humor about life, you can go anywhere on earth and have a good time. Someone has said that laughter is the shortest point between two people. It is the best way to break the ice, to cut the tension, to settle a quarrel, or to liven up a boring meeting. Laughter is a universal language that needs no translator.

It may surprise you to know that some of God's greatest saints loved to laugh. Martin Luther said, "If you aren't allowed to laugh in heaven, I don't want to go there." He also said, "If the earth is fit for laughter then surely heaven is filled with it. Heaven is the birthplace of laughter." The great English preacher Charles Haddon Spurgeon laughed so much that when a parishioner reproached him for using too much humor in his sermons, he replied, "If only you knew how much I held back!" C. S. Lewis used to say that his favorite sound in all the earth was hearty male laughter.

By the way, can you name the first two people recorded in the Bible who laughed? It was Abraham and Sarah who laughed (at God!) when they heard they were going to have a baby in their old age. They thought God was playing a joke on them. I take it that laughter is one of God's gifts to the human race. It keeps us from taking life too seriously—as if it all depends on us. Ed Howe said it this way: "If you don't learn to laugh at trouble, you won't have anything to laugh at when you grow old." Yes, there is a time to laugh, and laughter is a blessing from God as we endure the travails of this temporary world.

Father, thank You for the healing gift of laughter. I pray for a sanctified sense of humor today. Amen.

—✳—

SHINING THE LIGHT

✳ Do you think Jesus had a sense of humor? Do you agree with Martin Luther that heaven is the birthplace of laughter?

✳ Why is laughter so important in handling the trials of life?

—✳—

MORE LIGHT FROM GOD'S WORD

Read Genesis 21:1–7; Psalm 126:1–3; and Luke 6:21.

Twenty-Six

*

A TIME FOR WAR . . .

A time to search and a time to give up, a time to keep and a time to throw away, a time to tear and a time to mend, a time to be silent and a time to speak, a time to love and a time to hate, a time for war and a time for peace.

Ecclesiastes 3:6–8

For generations Christians have struggled to reconcile their faith with the terrible demands of war. The biblical perspective seems to be that war is sometimes in the will of God.

I realize that to say that war may sometimes be in the will of God is to jump into a firestorm of controversy. Such a view is not popular today. I ate lunch with several fellow pastors and heard one of them say emphatically that war is always a sin.

Let me say that I think my pastoral friend is partly right and partly wrong. War is terrible in all its aspects, and I would never want to be known as someone who is "for" war. I'm not even sure what a statement like that would mean. I don't know any sane person who is for war.

I think my friend is right to this degree: Wars come about because of the sinfulness of the human race. Warfare comes from the fallen nature of man. Whenever two nations go to war, sin is never absent. There may be sins of pride and oppression, or there may be sins of brutality and naked aggression, but sin is always part of the equation.

I would go a step further and say that there is rarely a war so "pure" or "clean" that one side is totally right and the other side is totally wrong. Even where such a case exists, there will almost always be some wrong motives on both sides.

But is going to war always and in every case sinful? I think not. Just before the Persian Gulf conflict started, Billy Graham said, "There come times when we have to fight for peace. Unfortunately, that's been true of the whole history of the human race." That doesn't make every war right, but it does mean that some wars are indeed justified in the eyes of God.

Better days are coming. In the last days God's kingdom will finally be established on the earth and all the nations will be at peace. The law of the Lord will go forth from Jerusalem and the Lord Jesus Himself will settle the disputes that today end in war. So wise will be His rule that weapons of war will become obsolete. People will take their tanks and turn them into combines; their cruise missiles will become tractors; B-52 bombers will be melted down and transformed into solar-powered water purifiers. Bullets will become obsolete. All the gas masks will be thrown away. They won't be needed in the kingdom Jesus will establish.

Best of all, the nations will not take up swords against

one another. The old spiritual says it very well: "Gonna lay down my sword and shield, down by the riverside. Ain't gonna study war no more."

That's how God intended it to be. Between now and then, nations will still go to war, but let us keep our eyes on the goal and let us work and pray for that day of lasting peace to come.

Prince of Peace, show me what it means to be a peacemaker in a world filled with war. Amen.

———❋———

SHINING THE LIGHT

❋ Do you agree that God has a place in His plan for everything—even war, sorrow, hatred, and death?

❋ Do you believe that war may sometimes be justified in the will of God? Under what circumstances would you as a Christian refuse to go to war?

———❋———

MORE LIGHT FROM GOD'S WORD
Read Joshua 23:9–10; Isaiah 2:2–4; and Romans 13:3–4.

✳

Twenty-Seven

GRASPING AT SHADOWS

What does the worker gain from his toil? I have seen the burden God has laid on men.

Ecclesiastes 3:9–10

When the final examination grades at Cambridge University were published, Henry Martyn's highest ambition had been realized. He was the honors man of the year. Strangely, his first sensation was keen disappointment. "I obtained my highest wishes," he said, "but was surprised that I had grasped a shadow."

This is part of the "burden" that seemed to dog Solomon's steps. Everywhere he turned he found more evidence that nothing in this life seems to satisfy. Even the highest achievements often leave us feeling empty. Missionary friends wrote recently that upon completing the translation of the New Testament into a tribal language they felt exhausted and depressed. Where was the feeling of satisfaction such a monumental achievement should bring?

There is another side to the story. A young man came to Christ on the streets of Chicago. I had the privilege of baptizing him, knowing that he would go to prison for a crime committed before his conversion. Writing from a maximum-security prison, he offered my congregation these words of encouragement:

> I want you all to know that you and everyone at the church are in my prayers always. It isn't any easier out there. I just finished fasting for three days successfully. It was hard, especially not smoking. But I make it through the power of God. I really feel good about that. I mean I feel cleansed in my mind and stronger in the Lord. You all will always be in my prayers. Keep up the good work for the Lord. I got him covered in here. I'm starting with my cellie. God bless and thank you. Your brother in Christ, Shane.

Those words are remarkable, especially his statement that "it isn't any easier out there." Here's a young man in prison for up to fifteen years, yet he is fasting, praying, and setting out to win his cellmate to Christ. That kind of boldness comes only from knowing God personally.

I do not doubt that my missionary friends have gained a better perspective after their work of many years. And I'm sure that Shane has many rough moments awaiting him behind bars. Henry Martyn was right about one thing: We live in a world of shadows where the ultimate significance of a given day's work may be hard to see. If we trust our feelings, we will soon give in to despair. But true faith rises above feelings to declare that what we do for Christ will last forever.

Lord God, in a world of passing shadows, You are the ultimate reality. Fill me with grace that I might serve You with joy. Amen.

—✳—

SHINING THE LIGHT

✳ Why is it that our dreams when finally realized and our goals when finally achieved often bring less satisfaction than we had hoped—and often bring a sense of disappointment?

✳ What does this teach us about life and about God?

—✳—

MORE LIGHT FROM GOD'S WORD
Read 1 Kings 19:1–9; Jeremiah 2:13; and Mark 8:34.

※

Twenty-Eight

A GOD-SHAPED VACUUM

He has made everything beautiful in its time. He has also set eternity in the hearts of men; yet they cannot fathom what God has done from beginning to end.

Ecclesiastes 3:11

Ecclesiastes 3:11 contains good news and bad news. The good news is that everything has a purpose in God's plan. The bad news is that no one can figure out the good news, that is, what the actual purpose is. To make matter worse—from a human perspective—God has put "eternity" inside every human heart. That means there is something inside each of us that yearns to understand what life is all about.

Commentator James MacDonald points out that this verse teaches a high view of God's providence. He asserts that there is a beauty in the way the events of life fit together, like the successive cogs in a wheel, each fitting into its proper groove, with a steady movement carrying forward God's plan. It is as if Solomon is observing the grand machine with all its parts functioning in perfect timing. Solomon listens and hears no grinding, no jarring noises. "Beautiful!" he exclaims.

Admittedly, from our limited standpoint we see many things that in themselves seem far from beautiful.

Sometimes it seems as if there is no "grand machine," or if there is, it's badly in need of repair. But that's because we see things from a human level and not from God's point of view.

This brings us face-to-face with Pascal's famous statement that there is a "God-shaped vacuum" inside each person. God made us to know Him. He designed us so that we would want to know Him—and then He guaranteed we wouldn't be happy unless He Himself filled the void within.

Romans 1:18–20 describes the knowledge of God seen in creation and found to some degree in the heart of every person. When Paul preached in Athens, he complimented the Athenians by calling them very religious people. The city was filled with idols, including a shrine "to the unknown God." Anthropologists tell us that man by nature is incurably religious. There is something in him that drives him to seek ultimate meaning outside himself. He may turn to God or he may worship idols of his own making or the evil spirits of his ancestors.

That "something" inside him is put there by God. Augustine gave us this oft-quoted prayer: "You have made us for yourself, and our hearts are restless until they find their rest in you."

We see ugliness, but we know there must be beauty somewhere. Deep inside we yearn to know God and to understand His plan. Yet the more we search to understand the big picture, the less we truly know. So in the end we are left with God and God alone.

Lord God, in a world of hard questions, You are the one eternal answer. Thank You for having the answers, and may I trust in Your goodness when the answer is not clear to me. Amen.

— ✳ —

SHINING THE LIGHT

✳ Why would God put us in a world where we are guaranteed to end up frustrated? What possible divine purpose could that serve?

✳ What does your own "God-shaped vacuum" look like?

— ✳ —

MORE LIGHT FROM GOD'S WORD

Read Jeremiah 23:18; 1 Corinthians 2:16; and Revelation 6:12–17.

Twenty-Nine

LIVING IN THE HERE AND NOW

I know that there is nothing better for men than to be happy and do good while they live. That everyone may eat and drink, and find satisfaction in all his toil—this is the gift of God.

Ecclesiastes 3:12–13

Have you ever wished you could sit down with God and have a good talk with Him about your own life? Have you ever wished you could just look Him in the eye and say, "Lord, what do You want me to do?" All of us have moments when we want to hear God's voice or receive some definite sign regarding a relationship, a business decision, a career choice, or a major expenditure.

With all my heart I believe the following statement: God wants you to know His will more than you want to know it; therefore, He takes personal responsibility to see that you discover it. Knowing God's will is ultimately God's problem, not yours. Let that last thought sink into your mind for a moment. You've probably never heard it put that way before.

Let me suggest what this really means:

1. God can put you exactly where He wants you to be.

2. He can arrange all the details years in advance.

3. He can open doors that seem shut tight.

4. He can remove any obstacle that stands in your way.

5. He can take your choices and fit them into His plan so that you end up at the right place at just the right time.

6. He can even take your mistakes and bring good out of them.

7. He can take tragedy and use it for your good and His glory.

All He needs—the only thing He requires—is a willing heart. He just needs you to cooperate with Him. This doesn't mean that you won't have to make decisions. But it does take the pressure off, because it means that you can trust God to take your decisions and use them to accomplish His will in your life.

Proverbs 20:24 tells us that "a man's steps are directed by the Lord. How then can anyone understand his own way?" There is something hidden in the Hebrew text that you wouldn't know simply from reading the English translation. The word translated *man's* in the first phrase comes from a Hebrew word that refers to a mighty warrior, a ruler, or a potentate. Solomon means to say that even the steps of a mighty man are ordained by God. The word *anyone* in the second phrase comes from a Hebrew word that stands for the whole human race. We might paraphrase it this way: "If God directs the steps of the mighty, how then can an ordinary man understand his own way?" The answer is, he can't! That's the whole point of the verse. We're like a herd of sheep stumbling around in the darkness, bumping into things, tripping over ourselves, trying to find our way forward. We can't say for sure where we've come from, where we are right now, or where we're going to be tomorrow.

Only God can see the big picture of life. When you understand that truth, you can enjoy each day as it comes—and let God take care of the future.

Father, teach me the joy of the present moment and the pleasure of living in the here and now. Amen.

———✳———

SHINING THE LIGHT

* If you were given a sealed envelope containing the record of the next ten years of your life, would you open it? Why or why not?

* Are you satisfied with your life right now? Do you agree that knowing God's will is His problem, not yours?

———✳———

MORE LIGHT FROM GOD'S WORD

Read Psalm 119:105; Proverbs 20:24; and 2 Corinthians 4:7–8.

———— ✳ ————

Thirty

NOTHING LEFT BUT GOD

I know that everything God does will endure forever; nothing can be added to it and nothing taken from it. God does it, so men will revere him.

Ecclesiastes 3:14

I believe that God orchestrates the affairs of life—both the good and the bad—to bring us to the place where our faith will be in God alone. Slowly but surely as we go through life, He weans us away from the things of the world. At first the process touches only our possessions (which we can replace), but eventually it touches our relationships (which may not be replaced), our loved ones (who cannot be replaced), and finally life itself (which is never replaced). Then there is nothing left but us and God.

Through all this process our heavenly Father leads us along the pathway of complete trust in Him. Slowly but surely we discover that the things we thought we couldn't live without don't matter as much as we thought they did. Even the dearest and sweetest things of life take second place to the pleasure of knowing God. In the end we discover that He has emptied our hands of everything and then filled them with Himself.

In writing these words I am keenly aware that I understand only dimly their full meaning. At this point in my life I still have many things in my hands: my wife, my three boys, my friends, my career, my health, my dreams, my plans for the future. But the process of growing older is nothing more than this—learning to hold lightly the things God has given you, knowing that you can't keep them forever anyway. At any moment, He can take them away—one by one, two at a time, or all of them together. Or He could take back the life He gave me five decades ago.

If I have any advice for you, it is this. Learn to hold lightly what God has given you. You can't keep it forever, and you can't take it with you.

Some of you who read these words are in the midst of a great struggle in your life. You feel pressured about something and you don't want to give it up. But you must . . . and you will. I can't spare you the pain that comes in yielding your dearest treasures to God, but I promise you the joy will far outweigh the pain you feel right now.

Eternal Father, teach me to let go of the things I can't keep and to hold fast to that which lasts forever. Amen.

——*——

SHINING THE LIGHT

* Why must we "let go" before we can experience the fullness of God Himself? What happens when we try to "hold on" too tightly?

* How have you experienced this truth (of letting go or holding on) in your own life?

——*——

MORE LIGHT FROM GOD'S WORD

Read 1 Samuel 15:29; Psalm 33:11; and Revelation 15:2–4.

✳

Thirty-One

HERE COMES THE JUDGE

Whatever is has already been, and what will be has been before; and God will call the past to account.

Ecclesiastes 3:15

The wrath of God is a forgotten doctrine, even in the evangelical church. Part of the problem lies in our definition. When we use the word *wrath* we tend to think of uncontrolled anger. While that may be true of human wrath, it is far from the truth about God's wrath. Here's a working definition: God's wrath is His settled hostility toward sin in all its various manifestations. To say it is "settled" hostility means that God's holiness cannot and will not coexist with sin in any form whatsoever.

God's wrath is His holy hatred of all that is unholy. It is His righteous indignation at everything that is unrighteous.

Please note these distinctions. God's wrath is not uncontrollable rage, vindictive bitterness, or God losing His temper. The Bible says in more than one place that God is "slow to anger" (Nehemiah 9:17; Psalm 103:8). God never "loses His temper" the way we do.

Wrath is what happens when holiness meets sin.

Wrath is what happens when justice meets rebellion.

Wrath is what happens when righteousness meets

unrighteousness.

Wrath is what happens when perfect good meets pure evil.

Wrath is God's "natural" response to sin in the universe. He cannot overlook it, He cannot wink at it, He cannot pretend it is not there. As long as God is God, He cannot overlook sin. As long as God is God, He cannot stand by indifferently while His creation is destroyed. As long as God is God, He cannot dismiss lightly those who trample His holy will.

God's judgment on sin (in this life) is generally not of the fire-and-brimstone variety. That rarely happens. When God wants to judge a community or a nation, He simply lets sin take it natural course. If we insist on destroying ourselves, God says, "OK, go ahead and destroy yourselves. I won't stop you." He lets us go our merry way. The true judgment on the human race is that man has turned away from God and does not realize it.

What is the judgment of God when men turn away from Him? God "gives them up" to their own devices. He lets them follow their own desires. He doesn't try to stop their meteoric descent into the abyss. God "abandons" the human race by letting men reap what they sow. Nothing more terrible could ever be contemplated. When men "abandon" God in their thinking, God "abandons" them. He respects the choices we make. If a man or a woman decides to live without Him, He says, "Fine. You can live without Me. In the end, you'll be sorry. But if that's your decision, I'll respect it."

Righteous Judge, I pray for the grace to choose the path of righteousness today. Amen.

— ✳ —

SHINING THE LIGHT

* According to 1 Peter 4:17, where does God's judgment begin? On what basis will God judge unbelievers?

* In what sense is God's judgment also a sign of His grace?

— ✳ —

MORE LIGHT FROM GOD'S WORD

Read Matthew 12:33–37; Romans 1:24–32; and Revelation 20:11–15.

✳

Thirty-Two

ORIGINAL SIN

And I saw something else under the sun: In the place of judgment—wickedness was there, in the place of justice—wickedness was there. I thought in my heart, "God will bring to judgment both the righteous and the wicked, for there will be a time for every activity, a time for every deed."
Ecclesiastes 3:16–17

No doctrine of the Bible is as easy to prove as the doctrine of original sin." When I read those words by Donald Grey Barnhouse, they seemed to leap off the page. That's the doctrine that says that left to yourself, with no outside influence, whenever you have a choice, you'll always choose to do wrong. G. K. Chesterton said it this way: "Whatever else may be said about man, this much is certainly true: He is not all that he could be."

I'm sure I don't need to spend a great deal of time debating that point. Something has gone wrong with the human race, beginning with the first man and woman, Adam and Eve. No one can successfully deny that fact. We are not all that we could be. And no matter how much we boast of our technological achievements, the sorry story of man's inhumanity to man always grabs the front page.

Call it what you will—a twist, a taint, a bent to do

wrong. Or as one hymn writer put it, "Prone to wander, Lord, I feel it. Prone to leave the God I love." Somehow, somewhere, somebody injected poison into the human bloodstream. That's why, even when we know the right thing to do, we go ahead and choose to do wrong. Deliberately. Repeatedly. Defiantly.

There are many ways we might discuss this truth. We could discuss it in cosmic terms, or international terms, or national terms, or local terms, but I think it's better to talk about it in personal terms. What do you see when you look at the man or woman in the mirror?

One writer answered the question this way: "There is no [person] on earth who, if his secret thoughts were fully exposed, would not deserve hanging ten times in his lifetime." My comment is, only ten times? For I know that when I look into the mirror what I see is a man who all too often knows what is right but chooses to do what is wrong. And I freely confess that sometimes impulses come into my mind that, were I to follow them, would destroy me, my marriage, my family, my career, and even my life. And yet I still think about them and I still sometimes want to do those things.

Who among us would say differently? You think about things—and sometimes want to do things—that you know would destroy you if you did them. And sometimes you want to do them anyway. And sometimes—if we are honest we must say this—you go ahead and do them.

What is it that makes us repeatedly do that which can

only hurt us? It is our condition of original sin. We know what is right and yet we deliberately choose to do what is wrong. There is something in us that bends us toward evil. The apostle Paul admitted that even as a Christian he struggled with this sinful nature. (See Romans 7:15–25.) He concluded that ongoing deliverance comes only in God's work "through Jesus Christ our Lord" (Romans 7:25). Apart from God's grace there is no telling how much greater your sin and mine would be. With the apostle we can only thank God for His lasting gift of deliverance.

> *Lord God, what would I do without the imputed righteousness of Jesus Christ? He took my sin; I gained His righteousness. May I never lose sight of that blessed transaction that saves me from damnation. Amen.*

—✳—

SHINING THE LIGHT

✳ We know that God will bring all things to judgment. When do His judgments begin? Can you think of ways in which God judges the wicked and rewards the righteous even in this life?

✳ How can we hang on to our faith when we see the wicked triumphing?

—✳—

MORE LIGHT FROM GOD'S WORD

Read Malachi 7:2–3; Matthew 23:13–15; and James 1:27.

✱

Thirty-Three

THOUGHTS FROM THE GRAVEYARD

I also thought, "As for men, God tests them so that they may see that they are like the animals. Man's fate is like that of the animals; the same fate awaits them both: As one dies, so dies the other. All have the same breath; man has no advantage over the animal. Everything is meaningless."

Ecclesiastes 3:18–19

It would be easy to draw wrong conclusions from a casual reading of verses 18–19. Perspective is all-important. Solomon is not dealing with questions of eternal life or what we might more generally call the afterlife. For there is lasting meaning—eternal meaning—to life. Solomon is simply examining the facts of human existence versus the facts of animal existence. He concludes that for all our vaunted superiority, in one respect at least animals and humans are exactly alike: We both die.

Behind the problem of death lies the reality of sin in the universe. Before sin entered through Adam's disobedience, death did not exist. Where does sin lead? The answer is simple: When I sin, I die. Every time I sin, I die a little bit more. We sin because we think it will bring us freedom and life but we end up with bondage and death. "Sin entered the world through one man, and death through sin, and in this way death came to all men, because all sinned" (Romans 5:12). First there was sin, then there was death. It is an inexorable law of the universe.

Just open any newspaper and look at the obituary section. Recently I found these names in our local paper, name after name after name: Arlen . . . Canavan . . . Doohan . . . Hill . . . Knowles . . . Lane . . . Lyons . . . Mahone . . . Masco . . . Pelzer . . . Sheridan . . . Shubert . . . Small . . . Videka . . . Witzel . . . Yuris.

Every day a brand-new list, and names never repeated. Why? Because death reigns all over Chicago. But death also reigns for you and for me. If there is one thing about which we may be perfectly certain, it is this: We are going to die someday. We say nothing is as certain as death and taxes, but death is far more certain.

When you die, the coroner will fill out a death certificate. There's a space on that certificate that says "Cause of Death." If we understand the Bible, the answer is always the same: "Sin." Not sickness, not cancer, not an accident, not old age. Those are merely symptoms of the one great cause of death: Sin.

Holy Father, my iniquity is vast and my sins beyond counting. My only hope is in the blood of Jesus. Amen.

—✳—

SHINING THE LIGHT

✳ What is the clearest proof from your own life that you are a sinner?

* In what sense is man's fate the same as the animals? In what sense is it different?

— ✳ —

MORE LIGHT FROM GOD'S WORD

Read Romans 5:14; 1 Corinthians 15:21; and Revelation 21:4.

✳

Thirty-Four

UNANSWERED QUESTIONS

"All go to the same place; all come from dust, and to dust all return. Who knows if the spirit of man rises upward and if the spirit of the animal goes down into the earth?" So I saw that there is nothing better for a man than to enjoy his work, because that is his lot. For who can bring him to see what will happen after him?

Ecclesiastes 3:20–22

Sam is twelve years old and has been raised in a Christian home. One evening he crawls up on the bed and with tears asks a question that has been troubling his heart. "What if when we die, there's no God? What if we just die and then we can't think anymore?"

Death is so final that you can't help but wonder sometimes what if "nothing happens" when we die. How would you answer Sam's plaintive question? Since we will all die someday—and since the cemeteries are adding and not subtracting people—on what basis do Christians have a hope that goes beyond the grave?

Over the past twenty years I have conducted funerals for all kinds of people. Most of them have been older people, but occasionally I do a funeral for a younger person, and sometimes I have the sad duty to officiate at the funeral of a child or an infant. The circumstances vary, but this much is certain. At the moment of death the truth about individuals comes out. You can fake your religion most days, but you can't fake it when you stare death cold in the face. In that moment Jesus makes all the difference in the world. In the saddest moments I have seen the light of God on the faces of those who have lost their loved ones. Through their tears they smile because they know Jesus, and He has made all the difference.

Verses 20–21 have been attacked for teaching a sub-Christian view of the afterlife. The truth is, Solomon isn't dealing with the afterlife at all. He's simply pointing out that from an earthly perspective no one can say what happens when we die.

But from a heavenly perspective, from God's perspective, we do know. Jesus is truly the answer to death for all of us. As D. L. Moody lay dying he exclaimed, "Earth is receding; heaven is approaching. This is my crowning day." Many have felt that way as they came to the end of life. For those who know Jesus, death is the passageway that leads to eternal life.

Lord Jesus, I hasten toward the day when I will be with You forever. You died so that I might live forever. Amen.

—✳—
SHINING THE LIGHT

* How does our universal unease over death point to something greater? Is this "divine discontent" part of the "eternity" God has put inside every human heart—(Ecclesiastes 3:11)?

* What is your hope of living beyond the grave?

—✳—
MORE LIGHT FROM GOD'S WORD

Read Genesis 23; Psalm 23:4; and Hebrews 11:13–16.

Thirty-Five

✳

BROKEN HEARTS ON EVERY CORNER

Again I looked and saw all the oppression that was taking place under the sun: I saw the tears of the oppressed—and they have no comforter; power was on the side of their oppressors—and they have no comforter. And I declared that the dead, who had already died, are happier than the living, who are still alive. But better than both is he who has not yet been, who has not seen the evil that is done under the sun.

Ecclesiastes 4:1–3

I have a friend who serves as a missionary in a third-world country. Not long ago he and his family had to evacuate their home because of political unrest. Rebel forces swept the countryside, denouncing the corruption of the present regime and promising that things would change if they came to power. There would be food for all, good jobs, and economic prosperity. In due course the rebels overthrew the government and became the new leaders. What's it like now? A little bit worse. No one has a job, the average per capita income is less than a dollar a day, and all those rosy promises have been forgotten. To borrow a phrase from American politics, the pigs are still at the trough, only the skinny ones have replaced the fat ones. Otherwise, nothing has changed.

Solomon saw similar oppression and bemoaned the

corruption of his day. The poor were so downtrodden that it would be better if they had never been born. Job felt the same way (Job 3:3–10).

Because God is sovereign, we know that He will eventually win the battle with Satan. And God lives outside time; the victory is already won in eternity.

From our perspective the battle rages all around us, and all too often the bad guys seem to be winning. A friend whose marriage broke up because of infidelity has grown enormously in her faith, but one question troubles her mind: Why is her ex-husband doing so well? He seems to be so happy despite his sin. Why doesn't God judge him? It looks to her as if he's gotten away scot-free. I reminded her that every football game has four quarters. It doesn't matter who's winning in the middle of the second quarter or at the end of the third quarter. The only thing that matters is who's winning at the end of the game. I told her that as far as God is concerned, we're still in the second quarter. In the end her ex-husband will reap what he sowed. He will live to regret his sin, and if he doesn't regret it in this life, he certainly will regret it in the next.

This principle applies in every situation where we wonder if truth and justice will prevail. God's sovereignty guarantees the ultimate victory of good over evil. It's just that God's timetable and ours aren't the same.

Lord, if I can't change the whole world, help me to improve my little corner. Amen.

—✳—

SHINING THE LIGHT

✳ Have you ever personally experienced injustice? What did you do about it? What good things happen when Christians get involved in the problems of others?

✳ What could you be doing to make a difference?

—✳—

MORE LIGHT FROM GOD'S WORD

Read Exodus 23:1–9; Obadiah 10–15; and Matthew 25:40.

Thirty-Six

THE RARE JEWEL OF CONTENTMENT

And I saw that all labor and all achievement spring from man's envy of his neighbor. This too is meaningless, a chasing after the wind. The fool folds his hands and ruins himself. Better one handful with tranquillity than two handfuls with toil and chasing after the wind.

Ecclesiastes 4:4–6

Over three hundred years ago Jeremiah Burroughs penned a book that has become a Christian classic. The title tells the whole story: *The Rare Jewel of Christian Contentment.* He argues that true contentment involves accepting what God has given you with a grateful heart and at the same time refusing to accept the status quo. Believers are to be contented and dissatisfied at the same time.

This is a delicate balance not easy to find and even harder to keep. Solomon warns against going to extremes. On one hand envy of others drives so much of what we do. We see what they have and want to have it—and more besides. This drives some people to become workaholics, living to work instead of working to live. On the other hand it's easy to sit back, fold your hands, take it easy, and watch the world go by. The workaholic burns himself out while the lazy fool ruins himself—and his family and friends who try to pick up the pieces.

Much to be preferred is the moderation of verse 6. Better to have a little money in the bank and peace at home than to have a million dollars and a date in divorce court.

A hard-driving, Type A corporate attorney happened to see a commercial fisherman he knew from church one afternoon, legs dangling off the pier as he helped his two young sons catch crabs. "Why aren't you out there fishing?" he asked.

"Because I've caught enough fish for today," said the fisherman.

"Why don't you catch more fish than you need?"

"What would I do with them?" responded the fisherman.

"You could earn more money and buy a better boat so you could go deeper and catch more fish. Then you could buy a fleet of boats. Soon you'd be rich like me."

"What would I do then?"

"You could sit down and enjoy life."

"What do you think I'm doing now?" the fisherman replied.

This is not an argument in favor of indolence but a call for balanced living. The wise person realizes that some things matter more than other things, that your career is not the measure of your self-worth, that having more money can't replace the joy of spending time with people you love.

Contentment means that you have everything you need right now. If you needed more, God would give it to you. Work hard, but don't make work your god. When you want what you already have, you've discovered the rare jewel of contentment.

Father, I praise You that I have everything I need for this moment. Teach me to enjoy what I already have. Amen.

——✳——

SHINING THE LIGHT

✳ Do you agree that you already have everything you need for the present moment? Are you satisfied with how God has treated you lately?

✳ What does it mean to be content and yet dissatisfied at the same time?

——✳——

MORE LIGHT FROM GOD'S WORD

Read Psalm 37:16–19; Proverbs 30:7–9; and Hebrews 13:5.

* * *

Thirty-Seven

ALONE AT THE TOP

Again I saw something meaningless under the sun: There was a man all alone; he had neither son nor brother. There was no end to his toil, yet his eyes were not content with his wealth. "For whom am I toiling," he asked, "and why am I depriving myself of enjoyment?" This too is meaningless—a miserable business!

Ecclesiastes 4:7–8

Before you read any further, go back and read the above two verses again. Out loud. Now think for a moment. Who do you know that fits this profile? I think every person who reads this book knows at least one person like the man Solomon describes in verses 7–8.

Now that you have a name in mind, I'd like to describe this person. I think I know him well. I've met him many times. More than anything else, this man believes in the value of hard work and the inherent dignity of a job well done. He's probably married and has at least three children whose pictures he carries in his wallet. He loves his wife and thinks about her more than she knows. It's true he works long hours—often he's gone by six in the morning and doesn't come home until after seven at night.

The pressures at work are so enormous that it takes

him an hour or two to unwind, so he doesn't spend much time talking in the evening. He's so tired that it's all he can do to read the paper, watch a little television and then go wearily to bed. His blood pressure is too high, he knows he needs to exercise, his diet isn't the best, and sometimes he's irritable and snaps at his family—and regrets it later.

It's true that he works seventy hours a week, but he doesn't think of himself as a workaholic. He simply loves his job—and he's good at it. And thankfully, he's able to bring home a nice paycheck and to provide good things for his family. One of these days he plans to slow down and smell the coffee. But not today. He gulps his coffee and heads for the door before his family knows he's gone.

One evening he comes home and his family is gone. While he was at work, the kids grew up, his wife went back to college and found a career of her own, his children moved out, and now the house is empty. He can't believe it. The Board of Directors just named him CEO. Now there's no one to share the good news with. He made it to the top—alone. This too is meaningless.

Slow me down, Lord, lest I jump the tracks and ruin my life. Amen.

SHINING THE LIGHT

✳ Are you a workaholic? What would your family and friends say?

✳ Why do so many men feel that they have fulfilled their duty simply by bringing the paycheck home? Why are so many wives unhappy with husbands who feel that way?

MORE LIGHT FROM GOD'S WORD
Read Proverbs 13:22; 23:4–5; and 1 Thessalonians 2:10–12.

Thirty-Eight

TOGETHER IS BETTER

Two are better than one, because they have a good return for their work: If one falls down, his friend can help him up. But pity the man who falls and has no one to help him up! Also, if two lie down together, they will keep warm. But how can one keep warm alone? Though one may be overpowered, two can defend themselves. A cord of three strands is not quickly broken.

Ecclesiastes 4:9–12

There were more than a few tears, and more hugs than I had seen in a long, long time. Old friends laughed and cried, and someone said, "Welcome back."

Welcome back, indeed. It reminded me of the words of the psalmist, "How good and pleasant it is when brothers live together in unity!" (Psalm 133:1). Such unity is like oil running down the beard of the high priest or like the dew on Mount Hermon. It is a precious sign of the Lord's blessing.

I was called to the meeting more as a moderator than anything else. At the beginning I reminded the group that it is the truth that sets us free. (See John 8:32.) When the truth-telling began, so did the tears—not of anger but of sorrow and love and, yes, even tears of joy.

Then the hugging began in earnest. Big, enormous

bear hugs, the kind that almost take your breath away, the kind that says, "I love you and I'm going to hang in there with you and we're going to make it together."

More tears. And smiles. And a voice behind me, a man's voice, saying, "This is the work of the Holy Spirit."

More voices talking. Confessions of failure and doubt. Jokes shared about the hard times behind us. Promises made to each other.

"What can we do to help you?" one person asked. A good question, and it brought forth a good answer, "Just listen to me when I need to talk out my problems."

At the end of this special meeting we made three promises. First, to let the past be the past. Second, to lower our expectations of each other so we wouldn't be surprised when the others aren't perfect. Third, to hold each other accountable for our spiritual growth.

Then we held hands and prayed together. Every prayer came straight from the heart. When we finished there were more hugs, lots of laughter, gifts of love given to each one, and a sense that we had all been part of a miracle.

When I left, group members were still talking. The sound of joy rang in my ears as I walked to my car. The party was just beginning.

Lord God, I thank You for the blessing of good friends, and I pray for the grace to be a good friend to others. Amen.

---*---

SHINING THE LIGHT

* How many close friends do you have? Do they know how you feel about them?

* In what areas of your life could you use some help from someone else?

---*---

MORE LIGHT FROM GOD'S WORD

Read 1 Samuel 18:1–2; 20:12–17; Romans 15:5–6; and Ephesians 4:1–3.

Thirty-Nine

*

THINGS WE CANNOT CONTROL

Better a poor but wise youth than an old but foolish king who no longer knows how to take warning. The youth may have come from prison to the kingship, or he may have been born in poverty within his kingdom. I saw that all who lived and walked under the sun followed the youth, the king's successor. There was no end to all the people who were before them. But those who came later were not pleased with the successor. This too is meaningless, a chasing after the wind.

Ecclesiastes 4:13–16

Commentators disagree on the situation described in verses 13–16. Apparently a king, popular in his youth, had grown foolish in his old age (perhaps through carelessness or greed, or it could be nothing more than the toll of advancing years). He no longer listened to the advice of others. Along came a younger man—energetic, full of ideas, brimming with vitality, eager to lead the country into a brighter future. Eventually the king lost his throne and the young man took his place.

The people cheered and the nation prospered. Then it happened again. After years in office, many people were not satisfied with the now not-so-young king. His idealism had vanished—or so it seemed. His vision for the future had slowly dissipated, and all that energy had evaporated with the passage of time. In the end he seemed just like the man he replaced—old, out-of-touch, cranky and creaky, an anachronism, a relic of bygone days. So the people cried out, "Give us a new king." Although Solomon doesn't spell it out, we may be sure that another young man rose to the throne and the cycle repeated itself again.

There are many lessons here, including the obvious one that fame is fleeting. Today's heroes are tomorrow's bums. Our attention is short, our memories nonexistent, our only question, "What have you done for me lately?" There's nothing one can do about this but to accept reality.

As I noted in chapter 5, our local historical society hosts an annual cemetery walk. As part of this event, area residents dress in period costumes and act out the life stories of notable men and women buried in this particular cemetery. For three years I portrayed the famous evangelist Billy Sunday at his gravesite. Each year I pondered the fact that in his day Billy Sunday was one of the most important men in America. He preached face-to-face to over 100 million people—and this before the age of radio, television, public address systems, computers, and VCRs. Today the public at large hardly knows his name. Rarely does anyone visit his grave.

This is the way it is. Solomon's advice is, "You don't like the idea that you can be replaced? Get used to it." As the late French president Charles DeGaulle once remarked, "The graveyards are full of indispensable men."

This truth might make you depressed—and it probably will if you've been hoping to take the world by storm. Good luck, and don't forget to leave a forwarding address. Here's some free advice: Do your best each day. Don't fret over how you will be remembered when you are gone. Invest your life in the things that really matter, and let God take care of your reputation.

Spirit of God, deliver me from faithless fear about things I cannot control. Help me to do my best and then to leave the results with You. Amen.

—✳—

SHINING THE LIGHT

✳ Name some leaders in history (ancient or modern) who started well but ended poorly (or people who started with widespread support but ended up rejected and forgotten).

✳ How does the Christian gospel address the problem of the fleeting nature of earthly fame? (Hint: See 1 John 2:17.)

—✳—

MORE LIGHT FROM GOD'S WORD

Read Deuteronomy 31:6; Matthew 16:24–27; and 2 Timothy 2:2.

✳

Forty

WATCH YOUR MOUTH!

Guard your steps when you go to the house of God. Go near to listen rather than to offer the sacrifice of fools, who do not know that they do wrong. Do not be quick with your mouth, do not be hasty in your heart to utter anything before God. God is in heaven and you are on earth, so let your words be few. As a dream comes when there are many cares, so the speech of a fool when there are many words.

Ecclesiastes 5:1–3

God is in heaven and you are on earth, so let your words be few." This is more than just good advice; Solomon has stated a fundamental truth of the spiritual life. While reading the Book of Proverbs I stumbled onto another verse from Solomon that made me stop and think. It's a verse the Lord applied directly to me.

The verse is Proverbs 10:8: "The wise in heart accept commands, but a chattering fool comes to ruin." That's a wonderful picture, isn't it? A chattering fool. A simpleton with a dunce cap talking up a storm.

I once knew a woman like that. She had had a hard life and along the way something seemed to come loose inside her brain. Every time I saw her I knew I was in for a twenty-minute monologue. She wasn't complaining, really, just spouting nonstop talk. If you tried to interrupt her she would raise her voice and start talking faster. If she got you cornered there was no escape. I suppose you would call her a compulsive talker.

What's more, she came to church every Sunday and was as loyal as she could be. Whenever we had a church supper, she would be in there with the rest of the women talking ninety miles an hour. We became good friends, and many times I was glad to see her because when we talked I didn't have to say anything.

Something like that must have been in Solomon's mind when he wrote this proverb. A "chattering fool" is someone who just won't stop talking. And in context, it must refer to a person who always has an explanation, a reason, an excuse for not doing what he is supposed to do.

That's hard, isn't it? Just to do what you are told. Most kids have a hard time learning that. So do most adults. Our natural impulse when we are told to do something is to ask, "Why?" That presumes that unless we fully understand or agree, we don't have to obey. As a general principle, that kind of attitude will get you into trouble more often than not.

I've been thinking about that in my own life. All too often I talk as an excuse not to obey. When a soldier is given an order, the proper response is obedience, not discussion. There is a time to talk and a time to listen, and there is also a time to do what you are told. As Solomon says, when the time for obedience has come, too much talk makes you look like a chattering fool.

Lord, I pray for the gift of saying more with fewer words. Amen.

— ✳ —

SHINING THE LIGHT

* How do you cure a person who talks too much?

* Would other people say that you talk too much? What steps can we all take to become promise keepers and not promise breakers?

— ✳ —

MORE LIGHT FROM GOD'S WORD

Read Proverbs 10:8; Matthew 6:6–8; and 2 Timothy 2:16.

---

* ✳ *

Forty-One

HOW TO MAKE
GOD ANGRY

When you make a vow to God, do not delay in fulfilling it.
He has no pleasure in fools; fulfill your vow. It is better not to
vow than to make a vow and not fulfill it. Do not let your
mouth lead you into sin. And do not protest to the temple
messenger, "My vow was a mistake." Why should God be an-
gry at what you say and destroy the work of your hands?
Much dreaming and many words are meaningless. Therefore
stand in awe of God.

Ecclesiastes 5:4–7

And now, a word about worship. After considering so many of life's harsh realities, it's as if Solomon wants to remind us that through genuine worship we can come into contact with the living God. (In fact, Bible scholar Louis Goldberg describes Ecclesiastes 5:1–7 as a kind of interlude in the book.)

But even here there are warnings. When you worship, listen first (vv. 1–3). If you make a vow to God, keep it (vv. 4–6). Finally, stand in awe of God (vv. 7).

That leads me to share some good news and some bad news about your worship. The good news is you can worship God anywhere. I agree with those who say you don't have to go to church to worship God. That's true, and lots of people who go to church don't worship anyway. They come by force of habit or in order to see their friends. Worship is the last thing on their minds. You can worship anytime or anywhere as long as you catch a glimpse of God's holiness. When you see God, you'll worship no matter where you are.

That's the good news. The bad news is as bad as the good news is good. Although you can worship God anywhere, you cannot worship Him halfheartedly. There is no such thing as halfhearted worship. Oh, there's religious routine and repetitive ritual, but true worship grips the mind and heart and soul.

Once during a radio interview I was asked why so many church members seem apathetic about their faith. I told the interviewer it's because our churches are filled with people who don't believe in God. They are theoretical Christians and practical atheists. They give lip service to God but live as if He doesn't exist. They are apathetic because God bores them. But as Ravi Zacharias has pointed out, "When man is bored with God, even heaven does not have a better alternative."

During the dark days of World War II, William Temple, then Archbishop of Canterbury, declared in a radio address to the people of England, "This world can be saved from political chaos and collapse by one thing only, and that is worship."

Does that sound preposterous? Listen to his definition of worship: "To worship is to quicken the conscience by the holiness of God, to feed the mind with the truth of God, to purge the imagination by the beauty of God, to open the heart to the love of God, to devote the will to the purpose of God." If that is what worship really is, perhaps the archbishop was correct. Only worship can save us. And we will never worship as long as we are bored with God. And God will bore us until we get a glimpse of His holiness.

Holy Father, open my eyes that I might truly see You, and having seen You, to see myself as You see me. I pray to be holy as You are holy. Amen.

— ✳ —

SHINING THE LIGHT

✳ Why are some people bored with God? What is the cure for that kind of boredom?

✳ Describe the most meaningful experience you've had in the last few months.

— ✳ —

MORE LIGHT FROM GOD'S WORD

Read Deuteronomy 23:21–23; Judges 11:30–40; and Matthew 5:33–37.

✳

Forty-Two

LOST IN THE BUREAUCRACY

If you see the poor oppressed in a district, and justice and rights denied, do not be surprised at such things; for one official is eyed by a higher one, and over them both are others higher still. The increase from the land is taken by all; the king himself profits from the fields.

Ecclesiastes 5:8–9

Imagine a typical government bureaucracy in which layers of officials take care of each other and look the other way when corruption occurs. That is what Solomon seems to describe, and he is equally interested by those at the bottom and the top. When you see the poor oppressed, don't be surprised, he says. This is the way of the world and things never change. The people with power rip off the powerless—thus it has been; thus it shall ever be.

As with many other statements in Ecclesiastes, this is not a moral judgment, just a statement of reality. This is life "under the sun."

At the other end of the spectrum, the king profits from the fields. That is, the poor pay exorbitant taxes and the money filters upward as each official takes his cut. And the king gets the biggest cut. In this system everyone makes out pretty well except the poor fellow at the bottom of the heap. He starts out poor and stays that way.

Is Solomon asking us to accept this state of affairs? Yes and no. Yes, in the sense that we live in a fallen world and should not be shocked that people in authority abuse their trust to line their own pockets. On the other hand, if we lose our sense of moral outrage we become complacent and actually begin to accept as normal that which is morally wrong.

The fact that sin reigns in the human heart means that we'll never be rid of corrupt leaders, but that's no excuse for tolerating official misconduct. Proverbs 24:10–12 reminds us that we will be judged for what we have done to rescue those who are abused by others. The fact that we cannot help everyone doesn't mean we should not help anyone. There is a time to speak out, a time to protest, a time to write letters, a time to make phone calls, a time to hold a press conference, and a time to sign petitions. God may even call you to run for office so that you can make a difference in high places.

If you cannot change the world, do what you can where you are and let God take care of what you can't do.

Lord, I pray for the strength to do right when those around me are doing wrong. Amen.

—✳—

SHINING THE LIGHT

✳ Have you ever been asked to do something you felt was wrong to do? How did you respond? What happened?

✳ How can Christians keep a good testimony in a workplace where evil seems to be tolerated or even encouraged?

—✳—

MORE LIGHT FROM GOD'S WORD

Read Daniel 1:1–17; Matthew 5:13–16; and John 15:17–21.

Forty-Three

THE MONEY TRAP

Whoever loves money never has money enough; whoever loves wealth is never satisfied with his income. This too is meaningless. As goods increase, so do those who consume them. And what benefit are they to the owner except to feast his eyes on them?

Ecclesiastes 5:10–11

I wonder if Solomon looked in the mirror as he wrote these words. After all, he was the richest man in the world. Did he never have enough? Does anyone ever have enough? Come to think of it, how much is enough?

Those who live for money will be perpetually dissatisfied no matter how much they make. It's like the story of the man who asked the millionaire, "When are you going to stop working and start taking it easy?" Answer: "When I make enough money." "How much is enough?" "Just one more dollar." Money has a way of doing that to you. It's a narcotic—the more you have, the more you want.

But that's only part of the problem. As verse 11 points out, the rich person amasses a great fortune only to see others consume his wealth. Nobody keeps his money forever. Even the entrepreneur who corners the market in pork bellies will eventually have to sell them or see them rot in the warehouse. And as for admiring your wealth, how many cars do you really need? Or how many shoes can you wear? You can only eat one meal at a time. You can only drive one car at a time. The rest is just for show.

Have you ever read the little book of Haggai? It's all about what happens when God's people decide that money is more important than God. The prophet uses a picturesque phrase—"you earn wages, only to put them in a purse with holes in it" (Haggai 1:6). This is the Law of the Unproductive Harvest. It happens to us over and over until we learn that God will not be mocked. Why would God do this? He allows us to suffer the results of our wrong choices in order to get our attention, to convict us of sin, and to lead us to repentance. God knows how to ring your phone. He knows where you live and He knows how to reach your private line anytime He wants.

Joyce Baldwin speaks of the "moral paralysis" that keeps us from obeying God. Because we know what God wants us to do and because we don't want to do it, our lives are stuck in a kind of permanent spiritual neutral— we can't go forward or backward. We just stay where we are—miserable and unfulfilled. That won't change until we finally admit that God matters more than money.

God of every blessing, do whatever it takes to free me from loving money more than I love You. Amen.

—✳—

SHINING THE LIGHT

✳ What keeps you from obeying God? Where is the "moral paralysis" in your own life?

✳ What are you going to do about it?

—✳—

MORE LIGHT FROM GOD'S WORD

Read Haggai 1; Acts 5:1–11; and Revelation 3:14–22.

※

Forty-Four

LIFESTYLES OF THE RICH AND FRUSTRATED

The sleep of a laborer is sweet, whether he eats little or much, but the abundance of a rich man permits him no sleep. I have seen a grievous evil under the sun: wealth hoarded to the harm of its owner, or wealth lost through some misfortune, so that when he has a son there is nothing left for him.

Ecclesiastes 5:12–14

Whenever I am under pressure, worry, or have problems I can't easily solve, I toss and turn all night long. Meanwhile my sweetheart sleeps contentedly next to me, blissfully unaware that I doze off and wake up every fifteen minutes. Over the years I have tried many remedies—taking a hot shower, drinking a glass of milk, counting sheep, praying through my problems, reading a book, and watching TV.

I should mention these bouts with insomnia don't happen all the time—or even most of the time—but they happen often enough that when I read about the rich man of verse 12 I didn't think about someone else. I thought about me. So I sympathize with the rich man, even though I am not rich. The poor guy has trouble sleeping at night.

There's a real contrast in verse 12: "The sleep of a laborer is sweet, whether he eats little or much, but the abundance of a rich man permits him no sleep." The rich man is the classic Type A personality. Hard-driving, demanding of himself and everyone around him. A workaholic. Up early. In bed late. Stressed out. Worried about protecting his investments. Doesn't exercise because it's a waste of time. Doesn't eat right because he doesn't have time. Doesn't spend much time with the kids and wife because he's got a business to run. He's living on the edge with a time bomb ticking inside his chest.

And do you know the worst of it? He can't sleep. The poor fellow tosses and turns, adjusts the pillows, lies awake staring into space worrying about his investments and whether he can fight off that hostile takeover. This man eats, sleeps, and drinks his work.

In contrast, the employee who runs his computer system for him is sleeping just fine. And why not? He doesn't have the boss's money; he doesn't have his problems either. His wife sleeps beside him. She works to help make ends meet. Between them they do just fine. It's a good life, made better by the fact that they aren't driven by the fear of losing all that they have. He's not as rich as his boss, but he's a much happier man—and he has a better life. Best of all, he sleeps like a baby, because he's learned that being rich has nothing to do with having money in the bank.

Father of Glory, I pray to discover the true riches that are already mine in Christ Jesus. Amen.

— ✳ —

SHINING THE LIGHT

✳ How well did you sleep last night?

✳ How important is money in your life? Did you tell the truth when you answered that question?

— ✳ —

MORE LIGHT FROM GOD'S WORD

Read Psalm 127:1–2; Proverbs 27:23–27; and 2 Corinthians 9:6–11.

***

Forty-Five

DEATH: NOT THE FINAL WORD

Naked a man comes from his mother's womb, and as he comes, so he departs. He takes nothing from his labor that he can carry in his hand. This too is a grievous evil: As a man comes, so he departs, and what does he gain, since he toils for the wind? All his days he eats in darkness, with great frustration, affliction and anger.

Ecclesiastes 5:15–17

Death is never far from Solomon's mind. Some people might say he is obsessed with it. I think he would say that most of us desperately try to avoid it. We swiftly change the subject to something more pleasant. But we would be better off if we thought about our own death more often.

A sixteen-year-old girl lay dying in a hospital room. A close friend came by for a final visit, not knowing what to say. As he tells it, he must have looked dreadfully upset, for "She looked upon my worried and harried face and said, 'Don't be afraid.'"

That is the heart of the Christian theology of death. It is most profound when it is the dying who can say to the living, "Don't be afraid."

As a pastor I spend a fair amount of my time dealing with death. Hardly a day goes by without someone asking me to pray for a loved one who is dying. As I write these words, I can think of a half dozen people who languish in nursing homes and hospital beds. Several have heart problems, others do daily battle with cancer. Any of them may die before the week is out.

Meanwhile Solomon points out that we go as we come—naked. We've even coined a term that reminds us of how we came into this world. If a person has no clothes on, we might say he's wearing his "birthday suit." To add insult to injury, Solomon points out that you can't take anything with you when you die. The rich man dies like the pauper. Oh, the surroundings may be different, but the one is just as dead as the other. The rich man can't take his riches with him, nor will the poor man take his poverty. Both leave it all behind. Death plays no favorites.

Most of us, if we thought about it, would like to live a long time. Maybe not forever, but at least for many more years. It's only natural to feel that way. If given the choice, we would keep our families together so that death would not intrude.

In recent years Easter has become my favorite Christian holiday. When I was young, it was mostly a day to dress up and hunt for Easter eggs. With each passing year, it has become more meaningful. Open the paper and death stares out from every page. Death is everywhere. Where is the resurrection? Easter reminds us that death is not the worst. "Fear not," said the angel. "For he is risen" (Matthew 28:5, 6 KJV). And those who sleep in Jesus shall also see resurrection.

> *Lord Jesus, hasten the day when death shall die and I shall rise from the grave, never to die again. Amen.*

—— ✳ ——

SHINING THE LIGHT

✳ Do you believe in the resurrection of the dead? If so, how does this truth affect the way you view your own death?

✳ What will you "leave behind" when you die?

—— ✳ ——

MORE LIGHT FROM GOD'S WORD

Read Isaiah 26:19; Daniel 12:1–3; and Philippians 3:20–21.

* * *

✳

Forty-Six

WHISTLE WHILE YOU WORK

Then I realized that it is good and proper for a man to eat and drink, and to find satisfaction in his toilsome labor under the sun during the few days of life God has given him—for this is his lot. Moreover, when God gives any man wealth and possessions, and enables him to enjoy them, to accept his lot and be happy in his work—this is a gift of God. He seldom reflects on the days of his life, because God keeps him occupied with gladness of heart.

Ecclesiastes 5:18–20

Several months ago my wife and I ate lunch with some friends who were visiting from another state. When we started our meal I noticed that the husband looked more relaxed than I had seen him in a long time. I soon learned the reason for his calm demeanor. He heard a minister suggest a simple prayer for the beginning of each new day. The minister challenged his listeners to pray this prayer for twenty-one days straight. My friend, who I'll call Sam, said that he had tried it and that the prayer had made a profound difference in his life.

At that point his wife chimed in to say that she had noticed a drastic difference in him as well. Before he began the day with the prayer, Sam often returned home tense over things that had happened to him during the day. Now, she noted, Sam would come home relaxed and in a good mood. As I listened, I wondered to myself what kind of prayer could make that kind of difference. Later Sam explained that for him the key was to pray the prayer the moment he woke up—even before he got out of bed. He even said that he had awakened that morning at 4:30, so he prayed the prayer and then went back to sleep.

The prayer itself is the essence of simplicity. It goes like this: "Heavenly Father, You are in charge of everything that is going to happen to me today—whether it be good or bad, positive or negative. Please make me thankful for everything that happens to me today. Amen."

I think Solomon would heartily approve of those sentiments. When my friend told me the story, he emphasized how this prayer works. "It doesn't change anything outside of me, but it does change everything inside of me. My circumstances don't change, but my attitude does." And that's why he looked so relaxed when we ate lunch.

In our final verses of Ecclesiastes 5, the key word in the passage is God. Bible commentator Derek Kidner notes that Solomon mentioned God four times in three verses—each time to remind us that the secret of happiness is to receive whatever comes to us as sent from heaven.

That is the essence of Sam's prayer, to remember that all that comes our way arrives via heaven, from the loving God who is in charge. May I challenge you to pray Sam's "secret" prayer for the next twenty-one days? See if the

Lord doesn't work miracles inside your heart.

> *Heavenly Father, You are in charge of everything that is going to happen to me today—whether it be good or bad, positive or negative. Please make me thankful for everything that happens to me today. Amen.*

— ✳ —

SHINING THE LIGHT

✳ Are you a thankful person? How have you experienced joy from God even during hard times?

✳ Name the joy-thieves in your own life.

— ✳ —

MORE LIGHT FROM GOD'S WORD

Read Habakkuk 3:17–18; John 7:37–39; and 2 Timothy 2:20–21.

※

Forty-Seven

HE DIED TOO SOON

I have seen another evil under the sun, and it weighs heavily on men: God gives a man wealth, possessions and honor, so that he lacks nothing his heart desires, but God does not enable him to enjoy them, and a stranger enjoys them instead. This is meaningless, a grievous evil.

Ecclesiastes 6:1–2

In the first two verses of Ecclesiastes 6, Solomon tells a truly sad story. A man works years and years, climbing to the top of his profession. When he finally makes it to the top, everything is taken away from him. We aren't told what happened, but many explanations come to mind. Perhaps he had a heart attack or lost his health and was forced to retire early. Or it could be that one of his employees conspired with the board of directors to remove him from power. Or he might have been falsely accused of wrongdoing and publicly humiliated. Solomon's point is clear: God gives wonderful gifts but that doesn't necessarily mean that we will enjoy them.

This is one of the mysteries of life. No one achieves wealth without the blessing of God, yet no one enjoys wealth without God's blessing. Once again Solomon brings us face-to-face with the seeming inequities of life and the inescapable fact that God alone controls the course of human events.

In one of his books, Watchman Nee wrote that we approach God like little children with open hands, begging for gifts. Because He is a good God, He fills our hands with good things—life, health, friends, money, success, recognition, challenge, marriage, children, a nice home, a good job—all the things that we count at Thanksgiving when we count our blessings. And so like children, we rejoice in what we have received and run around comparing what we have with each other.

Yes, we are like children, and when our hands are finally full, God calls us: "My child, I long to have fellowship with you. Reach out your hand and take My hand." But we can't do it because our hands are full.

"God, we can't," we cry.

"Put those things aside and take My hand," He replies.

"No, we can't. It's too hard to put them down."

"But I am the one who gave them to you in the first place."

"O God, what You have asked is too hard. Please don't ask us to put these things aside."

And God answers quietly, "You must."

God's grace comes in many shades and variations. Sometimes we see His grace in the things He gives us; often we see it in the things He takes away. I hesitate to say that God always replaces what He takes with something better (though He does), because that might be misunderstood in earthly terms. Some losses cannot be calculated because the cost is so great. But of this much we may be sure: When God takes something from our hands, it is not an act of hatred—much less a quirk of cruel fate—but an expression of God's love as He leads us to a place where our trust will be in Him alone.

> *Gracious Lord, when I tempted to hold on too tightly, remind me that I never owned anything, because all that I have comes from You. Amen.*

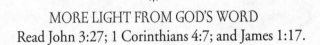

SHINING THE LIGHT

* What things in your life are you holding too tightly these days? Has God been asking you to let go?

* What must happen for you to loosen your grip?

—✳—

MORE LIGHT FROM GOD'S WORD
Read John 3:27; 1 Corinthians 4:7; and James 1:17.

※

Forty-Eight

STILLBORN MISERY

A man may have a hundred children and live many years; yet no matter how long he lives, if he cannot enjoy his prosperity and does not receive proper burial, I say that a stillborn child is better off than he. It comes without meaning, it departs in darkness, and in darkness its name is shrouded. Though it never saw the sun or knew anything, it has more rest than does that man—even if he lives a thousand years twice over but fails to enjoy his prosperity. Do not all go to the same place?

Ecclesiastes 6:3–6

Solomon's tale of woe continues. He speaks now of a man with a hundred children (meaning that he had economic security and that his name is certain to live on after he is gone), and he himself lives many years. Suppose the man lives two thousand years, Solomon argues. Surely that man should count himself happy and blessed.

Not so fast. What if that man cannot enjoy his prosperity and what if he doesn't have a decent burial? Well, then, it would have been better if he had never been born.

What's going on here? This man is rich, blessed with children, and he lives to a ripe old age. Yet he doesn't enjoy what he has and he dies either in misery or in shame or is somehow completely forgotten. Even his children don't care enough to give him a decent burial.

Solomon means to drive home the point that satisfaction is a gift from God. Contentment is a precious gift that not everyone receives. A person can have it all—and still be miserable and unfulfilled.

Jesus told a parable to drive home this very point (Luke 12:13–21). He spoke of a rich man who decided to expand his barns because he had so much grain that he couldn't store it all. Then he uttered these famous words: "And I'll say to myself, 'You have plenty of good things laid up for many years. Take life easy; eat, drink and be merry'" (v. 19). Little did he know that he would die that very night and someone else would own all his wealth.

I believe if Jesus spoke to a group of Christians struggling against today's materialism, this is what He would say: "If you want to invest your money, find the investment that will give you the most security and the best rate of return over the longest period of time. There is such an investment open to you. But it's not on earth. It's in heaven." (Review Matthew 6:19–24.) To "store up treasure in heaven" (6:19) means to live so that when you finally get to heaven, you won't be disappointed with what you see.

Those who have invested only in this world will be paupers in the next. Don't let it happen to you. What are you sending ahead to heaven? What will you find when you pass through the Jordan River on your way to the Celestial City?

O Lord, may I learn to value things in relation to eternity and to count as greater worth the prosperity of my soul than my prosperity in this world. Amen.

—✳—

SHINING THE LIGHT

✳ What occupies your mind the majority of the time?

✳ How would you spend $83,000 if you suddenly had that much "extra" money? What investments are you making today that will make a difference in eternity?

—✳—

MORE LIGHT FROM GOD'S WORD

Read Job 3:11–26; Matthew 6:19–24; and Luke 12:13–21.

✳

Forty-Nine

A WARNING TO WORKAHOLICS

All man's efforts are for his mouth, yet his appetite is never satisfied. What advantage has a wise man over a fool? What does a poor man gain by knowing how to conduct himself before others?

Ecclesiastes 6:7–8

His appetite is never satisfied." The Hebrew word translated "appetite" may also be translated as "soul." This is yet another reminder by Solomon that we were made for more than food. A man may get up, go to work, come home, go to bed, and then do the same thing for the next fifty years. After that he retires to Arizona, plays golf, and then he dies. So what? His soul has not been satisfied by anything he has done. He dies unfulfilled, even though his friends said nice things about him at his funeral.

As noted in *The Rare Jewel of Contentment* (Chapter 36), the workaholic, absorbed in his work, never finds deep satisfaction. Remember who the workaholic is? He or she is addicted to the job. For a workaholic, work is life; and the more one works, the better one feels. Here are three telltale signs that suggest you are prone to workaholism: First, your total energy is given to your work so that you have nothing left to give at home. Second, you constantly think about your work, even when you are not at work. Third, you find it difficult to relax when you are away from your work.

Workaholics generally are Type A personalities: Committed, aggressive, demanding, perfectionistic, goal-oriented, high achievers; impatient with weakness, easily frustrated, with enough stamina to work twelve hours a day, six (or seven) days a week. They love the long hours and the high-pressure job. One man said, "I don't know how I got rich. I only worked half-days: the first half or the second half."

From God's point of view, workaholics make three fundamental mistakes. To be more specific, they believe three heretical ideas: 1. "It all depends upon me." 2. "If I don't do it, nobody else will." 3. "My worth depends upon my work."

Like all heresies, there is a grain of truth in each statement. Work is good. It was created by God for the benefit of the human race (see Genesis 2:15). But to believe that your worth depends upon your work is to deny the truth of the grace of God. Workaholics are simply repeating the Galatian heresy—that we are saved by grace but kept by works (see Ephesians 2:8–9; Galatians 3:3).

The truth is, it all depends upon God. Everyone comes to that conclusion sooner or later. Unfortunately, some people have to die to find it out. Happy are they who understand the difference between living to work and working to live.

Lord God, when I am tempted to take matters into my own hands, grant that I may remember that Your way is always best. Amen.

———✳———

SHINING THE LIGHT

✳ How important is your job to your self-image? Have you looked to your work to satisfy the needs of your soul?

✳ When you have success, who gets the credit?

———✳———

MORE LIGHT FROM GOD'S WORD

Read Numbers 20:1–13; Job 40:1–14; and 1 Corinthians 10:1–12.

✳

Fifty

"TOO SHORT TO BOX WITH GOD"

Better what the eye sees than the roving of the appetite. This too is meaningless, a chasing after the wind. Whatever exists has already been named, and what man is has been known; no man can contend with one who is stronger than he.

Ecclesiastes 6:9–10

Solomon reminds us that God is *sovereign* and no one can argue with Him. Or as James Weldon Johnson reminds us: "Your arms are too short to box with God."

In the original Hebrew, the word *sovereign* is both a noun and verb. As a verb it means "to rule," and as a noun it means "king" or "master" or "absolute ruler." God's sovereignty means that He is in charge of the entire universe all the time. Sovereignty reminds us that God is God and we are not. When we think we're ready to advise God on how to run the universe, He just looks at us and says, "How many stripes do you have on your sleeve?"

It's like a person who visits my house and starts to criticize things. He doesn't like the color of the wallpaper, he doesn't like the decorations, he doesn't like the picture that hangs over the kitchen table. Once he is finished with his criticism, only one comment is appropriate. "Mister, whose name is on the title deed to this house? When you start paying the bills around here, you get a vote on the decorating. Until then, feel free to say nothing." When we recognize the rights of the Sovereign, we feel free to say nothing about the way God runs the universe.

Nebuchadnezzar, a pagan king, learned the truth about God's sovereignty the hard way. As he took a walk on the roof of the royal palace, the king began to say, "Is not this the great Babylon I have built as the royal residence, by my mighty power and for the glory of my majesty?" (Daniel 4:30). In that very moment God struck the mightiest man on earth. The great king lost his mind and began to run through the streets of Babylon, shedding his clothes as he went, bellowing like a cow. He made his way outside and began to live with the cattle. His hair grew long and his nails were like the claws of a bird. Seven years later he came to his senses (vv. 31–34).

Then the king gives us the moral of the story: "All the peoples of the earth are regarded as nothing. He does as he pleases with the powers of heaven and the peoples of the earth. No one can hold back his hand or say to him, 'What have you done?'" (v. 35): You will search through all sixty-six books of the Bible and you won't find a better statement of what God's sovereignty really means.

Let's take a lesson from a pagan king. All God's ways are just. And those who walk in pride He is able to humble.

Sovereign Lord, do whatever it takes to humble me so that I might experience Your power in my life. Amen.

—✳—

SHINING THE LIGHT

✳ Have you ever tried to deceive God? What happened?

✳ What area of your life would you least like for God to examine publicly?

—✳—

MORE LIGHT FROM GOD'S WORD

Read Psalm 51; 1 Corinthians 11:31; and 1 John 1:5–10.

Fifty-One

TRUE HAPPINESS

*The more the words, the less the meaning, and how does that
profit anyone? For who knows what is good for a man in life,
during the few and meaningless days he passes through like a
shadow? Who can tell him what will happen under the sun
after he is gone?*

Ecclesiastes 6:11–12

Life poses many questions that it does not answer. We
instinctively search for happiness, but we're frustrated by the fact that we don't know where to look. So we
spend our days running down one blind alley after another, desperately seeking something we can never find.

What's the meaning of life? In the first half of Ecclesiastes, summarized in verses 11–12, Solomon has considered the question from many standpoints: education,
pleasure, justice, prosperity, business success, busy activity, and being the king on his throne. He finds no satisfactory results and no lasting answers. Indeed, the longer he
looks, the more questions he has. Life is short, like a
shadow that disappears when the sun goes behind a
cloud. Everything about this life lacks substance. Then
we die, and who knows what happens then?

Would you like a happy life? The Bible says it is possible. Consider the familiar words of Jesus in Matthew

5:3–12, the verses commonly called the Beatitudes. Each of the Beatitudes begins with the word "Blessed." But the word translated "Blessed" actually means something like "deeply and profoundly happy." That throws a different light on this passage.

God says that the truly happy people of the world are those who have chosen to follow Jesus' teaching.

They are poor in spirit . . . but theirs is the kingdom of heaven. They mourn . . . but they are comforted. They are meek . . . but they inherit the earth. They are hungry for righteousness . . . then they are filled. They are merciful . . . in the end they receive mercy. They are pure in heart . . . as a result they see God. They are peacemakers . . . now they are called the sons of God. They are persecuted . . . but great is their reward.

Do you have the courage to be happy? "Courage?" you say. "What does courage have to do with it?" Everything. Happiness comes from making the right moral choices in life. Happiness is not a goal you seek; it's the by-product of seeking the right goals.

Happy are those who love the Lord.

Happy are those who put Him first.

Happy are those who respect God's laws.

Happy are those who are not ashamed of Jesus.

Happy are those who live according to the Bible.

They are blessed—and shall be the happiest people on earth.

Father, I pray for the wisdom to make godly choices that lead to true happiness. Amen.

—✻—

SHINING THE LIGHT

✻ Name three Bible characters who discovered that there is no lasting satisfaction in this life—and that ultimate satisfaction can be found in God alone.

✻ How would you answer the person who says, "Why bother searching if I can't find the answers I need?"

—✻—

MORE LIGHT FROM GOD'S WORD

Read 1 Chronicles 29:10–16; Matthew 11:1–6; and John 5:36–47.

---

*

Fifty-Two

LESSONS FROM THE FUNERAL HOME

A good name is better than fine perfume, and the day of death better than the day of birth. It is better to go to a house of mourning than to go to a house of feasting, for death is the destiny of every man; the living should take this to heart.

Ecclesiastes 7:1–2

Have you smelled the first shovel of dirt from your grave yet?" the friend asked the St. Louis businessman. The businessman, only forty-eight years old, knew that sooner or later he was going to die of cancer. Twice it had come to him, twice he had beaten it, but the third time he might not be so lucky.

We all wonder about life after death. It's natural to think about it, because sooner or later we're going to die. That much is certain.

Death is truly the last enemy of the people of God. That's not my word. It's what the Bible says in 1 Corinthians 15:26. We can beat many other enemies, but death always wins in the end. We can put it off, dress it up, delay it, or deny it, but to no avail.

A gifted colleague told me that the last year has been the most difficult in his life. His aged father died, his daughter-in-law died of cancer, then his wife of forty-four years died of a brain tumor after a two-year illness.

In his preaching he openly shares his personal journey through pain and suffering. I don't think I had gotten three minutes into my message on the providence of God before he put his head on the table and started to weep.

Afterwards he gripped my shoulder and said, "I believe all that, but it's so hard." He said that at the end, his wife didn't even recognize him. A hundred times a day she would say, "Who are you?" He wept as I have not seen a man weep in many years.

Jesus wept too. When He stood before the tomb of Lazarus He wept openly. People have wondered why He wept since He knew He was going to raise Lazarus from the dead. I think He wept because He loved Lazarus and because He felt the pain of death. He saw the grief of Mary and Martha and wept for all the suffering that death causes in the world.

Death is the last enemy, and until it is destroyed, we, like Jesus, will weep too.

Heavenly Father, thank You for the lessons learned in the house of mourning. I look forward to the day tears will be forever banished. Amen.

—✳—

SHINING THE LIGHT

✳ Under what circumstances can a person's death be considered a joyful event? A tragic event?

✳ Suppose you were to die today; what phrase would sum up your life so far?

— ✳ —

MORE LIGHT FROM GOD'S WORD

Read Lamentations 3:1–33; Mark 5:21–43; and 2 Timothy 4:7–8.

✳

Fifty-Three

WHY ANGELS FLY

Sorrow is better than laughter, because a sad face is good for the heart. The heart of the wise is in the house of mourning, but the heart of fools is in the house of pleasure.

Ecclesiastes 7:3–4

Somewhere I read that angels fly because they take themselves lightly and God seriously. This makes perfect sense to me. I can't fly—never have and never will—because like most people I take myself too seriously and God too lightly. In some ways I believe the greater challenge is not to take yourself too seriously.

Many years ago I heard Bible professor Vernon Grounds say that when approaching any important decision you should ask, "What difference will this make in 10,000 years?" What a liberating way to look at life. Ninety-nine percent of what you worried about this week won't matter three weeks from now, much less ten thousand years from now. In the year 2085—if Christ has not yet returned—it won't matter where you went to college or what kind of car you drove. But what will matter is that you have decided to take God seriously in every area of your life. All these trivial, piddling details that just soak up so much energy will in that day be seen for what they really are—trivial, piddling details.

That's why the wise spend time in "the house of mourning." When you view the body of a friend or loved one, it's amazing how so many of the lesser issues of life suddenly melt away. Moses declared of God, "You sweep men away in the sleep of death; they are like the new grass of the morning—though in the morning it springs up new, by evening it is dry and withered" (Psalm 90:5).

Recently when the death of a local pastor was announced on the radio, one of my friends heard only part of the report. He thought they were talking about me. It could have been me, it might be me next time, and certainly one day it will be me. Thinking along those lines certainly causes you to ponder your own mortality. Visiting the house of mourning reminds us that life is short and we shouldn't take ourselves too seriously. Enjoy each day as a gift from God and don't forget that you won't be here forever.

Lord, deliver me from the pomposity of taking myself too seriously and from the folly of taking You too lightly. Amen.

—✳—

SHINING THE LIGHT

✳ Think about the issues that have dominated your time lately. Which ones will really matter one thousand years from now?

* Which ones probably won't matter in ten years or ten months or ten weeks or ten days?

— * —

MORE LIGHT FROM GOD'S WORD
Read Psalms 119:71; 126:5–6; and Hebrews 12:5–11.

Fifty-Four

✳

THE HEALING POWER
OF HARD TRUTH

It is better to heed a wise man's rebuke than to listen to the
song of fools. Like the crackling of thorns under the pot, so is
the laughter of fools. This too is meaningless.

Ecclesiastes 7:5–6

I note that Solomon says it is "better" to heed a wise
man's rebuke. Better, but not easier. Most days I'd
much rather listen to the song of fools. I can do that by
turning on the radio and flipping across the dial. But a
wise man's rebuke? That's harder to find—and harder to
take.

Over the years I've been on both sides of that issue.
Sometimes I've had to confront another person about his
behavior. No matter how many times I've done it, I still
dread picking up the phone and saying, "Could we get
together? I've got something I need to talk about." I
much prefer to be the bearer of good news—to be the
one who says, "Congratulations! You just won $10 mil-
lion," rather than, "I'm here to repossess your car."
Knowing that people sometimes shoot the messenger
who brings the bad news, I'd rather not bring it at all. But
sometimes there is no other option.

As I look across the years, I can see clearly that when
I have made that phone call anyway, the results have al-

most always been positive in the long run. To be sure, the initial reaction is often anger and denial; but where a bond of friendship and love exists, hard truth can be told. And when the truth is finally faced, it sets us free, just as Jesus said it would (John 8:32).

Sometimes I've been on the receiving end of a wise man's rebuke. The hardest part of receiving a rebuke is discerning whether or not it comes from a wise person; it may be from a cranky critic. I'm not always a good judge of that—since I don't have the gift of discernment—but I have close friends who can help me sort things out, keeping the fish and throwing away the bones.

None of this is easy or pleasant—whether rebuking or being rebuked—but both are absolutely necessary for healthy spiritual growth. God repeatedly puts us in places where we have to speak the truth and where we have to hear the truth. Blessed are the truth-tellers—and the truth-hearers—for they shall be set free.

Lord, thank You for friends who care enough to tell me the hard truth. I pray for grace to hear Your voice through their words. Amen.

—✻—

SHINING THE LIGHT

✻ When was the last time you were rebuked by someone you know? How did you respond?

* Which is harder for you—to rebuke a friend or to be rebuked by a friend?

— * —

MORE LIGHT FROM GOD'S WORD

Read Proverbs 9:8; 27:5; Galatians 6:1–5; and James 5:19–20.

* * *

Fifty-Five

KEEP YOUR COOL

Extortion turns a wise man into a fool, and a bribe corrupts the heart. The end of a matter is better than its beginning, and patience is better than pride. Do not be quickly provoked in your spirit, for anger resides in the lap of fools.

Ecclesiastes 7:7–9

Certain things ought to make us angry. Extortion is a good example, and so is bribery. Psalm 4:4 reminds us that anger and sin live next door to each other. While it is possible to be angry without sin, it isn't easy to stay angry without crossing the line into forbidden territory. The key is learning to control your own spirit. Ecclesiastes 7:9 shows us one of the primary signs of a fool: He can't control his temper. If you cross him, he is "quickly provoked." In modern parlance, he has a short fuse.

I stopped at a local auto dealership one time, met the manager, and told him I was thinking about leasing a car. We chatted briefly, and then he began showing me one of the models in the showroom. He was obviously proud of the car because he went on and on about front disc brakes, front-wheel drive, overhead cams, tune-ups that last 30,000 miles, and the all-important galvanized steel body. He was thirty-something, personable, and a walking encyclopedia of knowledge about his product.

We started with the left rear of the car and he had talked his way along the side and under the hood when I heard a noise behind me. People were talking loudly but I couldn't quite make out what they were saying. No matter. The manager just kept on rolling about the turbo-charged pistons, or whatever.

The voices got louder until I couldn't help but turn and look. Two people, a young man in his early twenties and a lady slightly older (and taller), were screaming at each other. I think maybe she had something to do with the payroll, and maybe he was angry because he wasn't getting his check. She screamed something about him being a low form of life, and he shouted back a similar compliment. She made a reference to fertilizer, and he answered in the same vein.

And all this happened while we—myself and the others in the showroom—looked on. It was ugly and scary because I thought they were going to come to blows. I hadn't seen people get angry in public like that in a long time.

The most amazing fact is that the manager never stopped talking. Even while they were cursing each other twenty feet away, he bragged about the transverse-mounted engine and the gas-filled struts. I didn't hear a word of it. He had me sit down in the driver's seat, but I didn't feel a thing. We went outside to look at another model but I didn't see a thing.

All the way home all I could think of was what I had just experienced—the ugly words, the bitterness, all that verbal venom flying through the air. That man and woman were like two fools in combat, armed with weapons of outrage. I bought my next car somewhere else.

Consider the power of anger. It overcomes a thousand well-spoken words.

Father, I pray for the spirit of Jesus to fill my heart so that I might learn how to respond with grace under pressure. Amen.

—✳—

SHINING THE LIGHT

✳ Name three situations that tend to make you "provoked in your spirit." Would an objective person say that you have a problem with anger?

✳ Can you think of anything foolish you've done while angry?

—✳—

MORE LIGHT FROM GOD'S WORD

Read Proverbs 16:32; James 1:19; and 1 Peter 2:21–23.

Fifty-Six

———— ✳ ————

LONGING FOR THE GOOD OLD DAYS

Do not say, "Why were the old days better than these?" For it is not wise to ask such questions. Wisdom, like an inheritance, is a good thing and benefits those who see the sun. Wisdom is a shelter as money is a shelter, but the advantage of knowledge is this: that wisdom preserves the life of its possessor.

Ecclesiastes 7:10–12

Memory is a good thing, if you remember the right things at the right times. For a husband to recall his wedding vows while on a business trip may keep him from making a life-destroying mistake. By the same token, a wife who remembers that her marriage has had many good moments may resist giving up in despair. In one sense the fountain of gratitude flows from a good memory. We will be thankful if we recall how much we have been given and how little we have deserved our many blessings. Thus did David exhort the children of Israel to recount God's good deeds and to let that memory be a bulwark in the present hour of crisis.

But there is a kind of memory that hinders our spiritual progress. Sometimes a painful event from the past keeps you from moving ahead. Easing that painful memory may require choosing to forgive, even though the other person won't admit he or she did anything wrong. It often will require deliberately choosing to let go of some dream you held onto for many years. No matter what it is, whether good or bad, if it's holding you back, you've got to let go of it.

The same thing happens to us whenever we play the comparison game. We compare our children and our wives and husbands. We compare what we used to have with what we have now. We remember the past as better than it really was so that the present seems worse than it really is.

The comparison game is foolish and dangerous because only God can make a proper comparison. I am reminded of that strange and touching conversation between Jesus and Peter in John 21. Three times Jesus asked, "Do you love me?" Three times Peter answered yes. Three times Jesus told him to feed the flock of God. Then Peter saw John following them and asked, "What about him?"—meaning, "Where does John fit in your plans?" To which Jesus replied, "If I want him to remain alive until I return, what is that to you?" (John 21:22).

God isn't obligated to treat us in exactly the same way He treats anyone else, nor is He required to treat us today exactly as He did yesterday. Because God is God and we are not, He has the absolute right to do as He pleases. If you think about that fact, it renders all comparisons useless and counterproductive.

Spirit of Grace, I thank You for the promise of better things to come for the people of God. Amen.

—✳—

SHINING THE LIGHT

✳ What are the "good old days" for you? If you could go back and relive them again, would you?

✳ What's the difference between remembering the past and living in it?

—✳—

MORE LIGHT FROM GOD'S WORD

Read Psalm 77:1–10; 2 Corinthians 6:2; and 2 Peter 3:10–13.

Fifty-Seven

✳

THE STEPS AND THE STOPS OF LIFE

Consider what God has done: Who can straighten what he has made crooked? When times are good, be happy; but when times are bad, consider: God has made the one as well as the other. Therefore, a man cannot discover anything about his future.

Ecclesiastes 7:13–14

We had just finished a grand eleven-day tour of the Holy Land and then boarded a jet for a final two-day visit to Greece. We made it as far as the Athens airport with no major problems. Then the unexpected happened: Two of the members of our group were detained by the Greek customs officials because their passports contained invalid visas.

To those who never travel overseas that may not sound serious, but it is. A visa is a legal document that allows a person to enter a foreign country for a designated period of time (a few days or weeks or months). No visa, no entry—it's really as simple as that. To make matters worse, when you are standing in the airport of another country waiting for the customs officer to clear you, there really isn't anything you can do to help the situation along. If you lose your temper, your papers have a mysterious way of being misplaced for hours at a time.

So there we were, waiting and wondering what would happen next. After several conversations, it all came down to this: The customs officials would send a telex to the head office in downtown Athens and wait for a decision—which would take four or five hours at least. The rest of our group could go ahead to the hotel, but the two women would have to stay in the airport.

I wondered how they would react to this frustrating delay. One of the women smiled at me and quoted Psalm 37:23 (KJV), "The steps of a good man are ordered by the Lord." Then she added this phrase—"And so are the stops."

What a fantastic insight that is. Both our steps and our stops are ordered by the Lord. He is in charge of everything that happens to us, and that definitely includes those maddening delays that seem to come out of nowhere. Sometimes we end up sitting for hours on a bench when we could be doing something productive—or so we think.

But it's exactly at that point that our faith must rise to the challenge. Do you believe that God has a plan for your life that includes every little detail? Do you believe that God is working out that plan every moment of every day? And do you believe that God is able to use everything that happens to you for your good and His glory?

If all of that is true, then even in the stops of life we can still give thanks to God. That doesn't make "stopping" easy or pleasant, but it does release us from the urge to barge ahead in our own strength.

Are you temporarily "stopped" right now? Fear not, child of God. This is part of His divine appointment for you. Wait on the Lord and soon enough your stopping will become stepping.

Lord of time and eternity, if I should have less than I want today, may I be content in the knowledge that I already have everything I need. Amen.

— ✳ —

SHINING THE LIGHT

✳ If you could change one situation in your own life right now, what would it be? If you could ask one question about your future, what would it be?

✳ Do you truly believe that God has ordained your hard times as well as your good times?

— ✳ —

MORE LIGHT FROM GOD'S WORD

Read Exodus 16:31–35; Philippians 4:11–13; and 1 Timothy 6:6–10.

———— ✳ ————

Fifty-Eight

LIVING IN THE GOLDEN MEAN

In this meaningless life of mine I have seen both of these: a righteous man perishing in his righteousness, and a wicked man living long in his wickedness. Do not be overrighteous, neither be overwise—why destroy yourself? Do not be overwicked, and do not be a fool—why die before your time? It is good to grasp the one and not let go of the other. The man who fears God will avoid all extremes.

Ecclesiastes 7:15–18

This much-debated passage evidently means something like this: Don't try to impress God by acting like you're more righteous than you really are. God sees through the sham because His vision penetrates to the heart. You can't control the length of your days by acting super-religious. Sometimes the righteous die young while the wicked live to a ripe old age. This is a true mystery.

So what does it mean to be "overrighteous"? Louis Goldberg suggests that it means becoming overconscientious or superscrupulous about our daily lives. You can worry so much about the secondary details that you lose the joy of each new day. And what good is that—especially since you could die in the next six hours? Understood in this light, these verses are an Old Testament echo of Jesus' warning to the Pharisees in Matthew 23. They strained at the gnats of Jewish law only to swallow the camel of sinful pride and selfish indulgence. Don't overdo it, says Solomon, because if you major on the secondary details—which may in themselves be valuable—you risk cutting yourself off from family and friends. You can even end up destroying yourself.

On the other hand, don't be "overwicked" either. This means just what it says. Don't use your sinfulness as an excuse to sin even more. The fact that you aren't perfect should spur you on toward holiness, not toward moral compromise. It's easy to see how this line of reasoning might work. "I've already told one lie. What difference will another make?" Or "I know I shouldn't have used foul language, but why stop now?" All such reasoning is evil. Why compound your troubles by continuing to sin? When you're in a hole, stop digging.

I recall the sage advice of an old friend who said, "If you can't make things better, at least make sure you don't make them worse." This applies to all of us because everyone struggles with sin to one degree or another. You don't have to take another drink, you don't have to cheat a second time, you don't have to keep on swearing, and you don't have to lose your temper over and over again. By the power of God, and with the help of a few good friends, you can stop the patterns of sin and replace them with habits of holiness.

Seen in that light, this passage offers excellent advice for the spiritual life. Don't be something you're not and don't make matters worse than they already are. This is the "Golden Mean" of the righteous life.

> *I confess that I am often confused by the things I see around me. Turn my heart, gracious God, from the uncertainties of this life to an eternal interest in Jesus Christ. Amen.*

—✳—

SHINING THE LIGHT

✳ Can you think of any examples (ancient or modern) of good men who died too young and evil men who lived much too long? Why would God allow such an apparent inversion of moral justice?

✳ Are you more likely to be "overrighteous," "overwise," or "overwicked"?

—✳—

MORE LIGHT FROM GOD'S WORD

Read 1 Kings 21:1–14; Jeremiah 12:1–5; and 1 Corinthians 3:18–20.

—— ✳ ——

Fifty-Nine

BLESSED FORGETFULNESS

Wisdom makes one wise man more powerful than ten rulers in a city. There is not a righteous man on earth who does what is right and never sins. Do not pay attention to every word people say, or you may hear your servant cursing you— for you know in your heart that many times you yourself have cursed others.

Ecclesiastes 7:19–22

There is a vast difference between knowledge and wisdom. College can give you knowledge, but it won't necessarily give you wisdom. You have to pick that up on your own. Which is not to say that you can't get wisdom in college, only that it doesn't come as a fringe benefit of paying your tuition. Biology is the science of life; wisdom is the understanding of life. That roughly is the difference between knowledge and wisdom. You need both to be successful.

Verse 19 tell us that wisdom elevates a person above his contemporaries. Those who have it will rise to the top. Solomon suggests that we take ten men—any ten men—and study them carefully. Then consider one truly wise man. That one wise man will in his wisdom be more powerful than the ten men with their accumulated knowledge.

Solomon also reminds us that we're all sinners and then applies that truth in an unexpected way: Don't pay attention to everything others say about you. That much we've heard before, and it stands as a piece of good advice. People are going to criticize you no matter what you do. My mother taught me to say, "Sticks and stones may break my bones but words will never hurt me." That's not always true. Words do hurt, sometimes much worse than broken bones.

Sometimes it pays to be a little hard of hearing. The reason may surprise you: "You may hear your servant cursing you." Just substitute "your roommate" or "your fellow-worker" or "your best friend," and you get the basic message.

Don't pay too much attention to what people say, because if you do, you will sooner or later hear people say things about you that hurt you deeply. What will you do then? Hearing a critical comment may not be helpful because it can lead to all sorts of wrong conclusions. The key is the word *cursing*. You will hear your servant cursing, lose your cool and wonder, *Why is my servant cursing me?* You end up losing your peace of mind and may in fact be tempted to lash out in blind anger.

When other people fail him, the wise man remembers that he himself has failed others many times. That one fact will produce a wonderful quality in your life—patience. You can't have wisdom without it.

It matters not where you are or who you are or what you do. People will fail you. Your best friends will fail you. Your coworkers will fail you. Your brothers and sisters will fail you. Your parents will fail you. If you live long enough, everyone you count dear in life will fail you sooner or later.

The wise person remembers that he too has failed many times.

Remembering that will temper your anger.

Remembering that will keep you from rash decisions.

Remembering that will help you hold your tongue.

God of righteous judgment, when I am tempted to strike back at those who have hurt me, remind me that I too am a sinner and prone to many mistakes. Amen.

———✳———

SHINING THE LIGHT

✳ Are you angry at anyone because they failed you? In what ways have you failed others?

✳ Take a moment and pray for the grace to control your tongue.

———✳———

MORE LIGHT FROM GOD'S WORD

Read 2 Samuel 20:14–22; Matthew 18:21–35; and 1 Corinthians 13:3–7.

✳

Sixty

LIVING IN THE VALLEY OF ACHOR

All this I tested by wisdom and I said, "I am determined to be wise"—but this was beyond me. Whatever wisdom may be, it is far off and most profound—who can discover it? So I turned my mind to understand, to investigate and to search out wisdom and the scheme of things and to understand the stupidity of wickedness and the madness of folly.

Ecclesiastes 7:23–25

That is really stupid!" Perhaps you've said those words about some policy in your local supermarket, bank, or even some act of congress. But do you ever consider how our own selfish acts are at times stupid? Take a moment to ponder the last two phrases of verse 25: "the stupidity of wickedness" and "the madness of folly." In what sense is wickedness truly stupid?

The foolishness of the wicked is not always obvious to them; their actions may even seem to them to make sense. Consider Hosea's unfaithful wife, a woman named Gomer. She had broken her marriage vows and chosen a life of repeated adultery. Time and again the prophet had appealed to his wife to come home. But she would not do it.

"I will go after my lovers," she said, "who give me my food and my water, my wool and my linen, my oil and my drink" (Hosea 2:5). Like the Prodigal Son who left his father for the "far country," she enjoyed the passing pleasures of sin. She loved the nightlife, the excitement, the parties, the food, the wine, and the late-night trysts. In her rebellious heart, she was done with the boring routine of daily life—no more picking up after the children, no more meals to prepare for an unappreciative family, no more listening to her husband quote Scripture day and night.

There are times in life when you have to let people make their own choices. Sometimes you have to love them enough to let them go—even if you know their choices will only bring them (and you) pain, sorrow, and deep regret. No one who has ever wept over a wayward child (or a wayward mate) can doubt the anguish of Hosea's heart as he watched his sweetheart destroy herself step by step.

Your loved ones can walk out on you, but they can never walk out on God. The Hound of Heaven will pursue them relentlessly, wooing them, convicting them, giving them just enough pleasure to make them miserable but not enough to make them happy.

Wickedness is truly stupid and sinful folly—nothing but madness—as Gomer discovered and as countless others have experienced over the years. Here is God's promise regarding His wayward children, made to Gomer and the children of Israel. "Therefore I am now going to allure her; I will lead her into the desert and speak tenderly to her. There I will give her back her vineyards, and will make the Valley of Achor a door of hope" (Hosea 2:14–15). The name "Achor" means "trouble" or "suffering."

God promises to lead His children into the valley of suffering, where they face the consequences of their own sins. Yet on the other side of the valley He will erect a "door of hope," where they can begin a brand-new life.

Holy Father, deliver me from thinking that the wickedness of others somehow makes me more righteous. Amen.

———*———

SHINING THE LIGHT

* What is your definition of wickedness? List three contemporary examples.

* What areas of wickedness can you find in your own life?

———*———

MORE LIGHT FROM GOD'S WORD

Read Deuteronomy 30:11–14; 1 Kings 3:5–14; and Romans 7:15–25.

✳

Sixty-One

TRAPPED IN THE NAME OF LOVE

I find more bitter than death the woman who is a snare, whose heart is a trap and whose hands are chains. The man who pleases God will escape her, but the sinner she will ensnare.

Ecclesiastes 7:26

If any man knew the dangers of sexual temptation, it was Solomon. After all, he had seven hundred wives and three hundred concubines. This may sound strange to us—perhaps even unbelievable—but three thousand years ago it would not have been thought unusual for an oriental monarch to have a vast harem. Having many women under your control was a sign of power and vast wealth.

Recently someone asked me why the Bible doesn't directly forbid polygamy. I answered that in the most basic sense, it does. When God created Adam, He didn't create Eve, Sally, Jennifer, and Kathy. God didn't create a harem for Adam and He didn't give Adam a choice either. In the beginning it was one man and one woman joined together in a binding, lifetime partnership called marriage (see Genesis 2:24; Matthew 19:4–6). This divine example rules out polygamy as God's highest and best plan for the human race.

So why then did God allow it? Perhaps for the same reason Moses allowed divorce—the hardness of the human heart. Even in cases where multiple wives advanced God's plan, such as Jacob's two wives and two concubines, there was jealousy and competition among the women. Solomon himself is the prime example. Despite the fact that Deuteronomy 17:17 explicitly forbids kings to have multiple wives, he repeatedly violated this scriptural principle. In the end his foreign wives turned his heart away from the Lord (1 Kings 11:1–4).

It is sometimes suggested that many of these marriages were made for purposes of establishing peaceful relationships with other countries. For instance, a king might marry a royal daughter from a neighboring empire, thus ensuring peace and free trade for many years to come. No doubt Solomon's multiple marriages contributed to the "golden age" of peace that Israel enjoyed during his reign. But in the end the price was too high. After his death the kingdom split and the nation slid into idolatry.

All of this may seem rather far removed from our situation. Most of us aren't faced with the temptation to practice polygamy. But we do face precisely the same temptation to lower our standards and to rationalize our disobedience. It's all too easy for us to justify flirtatious behavior, words spoken in secret, and prolonged sexual fantasies, whether we are married or single.

The wrong man, or woman, can turn us away from God. It happens gradually, imperceptibly, certainly without our conscious consent, just as it happened to Solomon. Slowly we begin to lower our standards—not just physically but spiritually and emotionally too. Soon our hearts have been given to someone who leads us away from the Lord. If you don't think this could happen to you, think again.

If we follow Solomon's bad example, we will discover the truth of his words. This world is filled with men and women who care nothing for God's truth. Let each person who reads this look into his or her own soul. What is the price of your purity?

Lord Jesus, You showed us how to stay clean in a dirty world. May Your life be my example and Your Word my guide. Amen.

—✷—

SHINING THE LIGHT

✷ How would you assess you own commitment to moral purity? What temptations do you face in this area?

✷ Are there any relationships that need to be broken in order for you to be clean before the Lord? Any relationships that need to be broken because they keep you from honoring God?

—✷—

MORE LIGHT FROM GOD'S WORD

Read Matthew 5:27–28; 1 Corinthians 7:2; and 1 Thessalonians 4:3–8.

✴

Sixty-Two

A BETTER WAY TO PRAY

"Look," says the Teacher, "this is what I have discovered: Adding one thing to another to discover the scheme of things—while I was still searching but not finding—I found one upright man among a thousand, but not one upright woman among them all. This only have I found: God made mankind upright, but men have gone in search of many schemes."

Ecclesiastes 7:27–29

Let's get one thing out of the way immediately. I don't think Solomon intended in verse 28 to make a relative comparison as to the worth of men and women in general. That wouldn't be fair and his conclusion wouldn't be right. Remember that Solomon was a consummate lady's man. How else can you explain the hundreds of wives and concubines—most of whom were foreign women whose religion was at odds with the worship of the living God? Among those women—those foreign women—he didn't find a single woman who could be called "upright."

The record for the men is not much better—one out of a thousand. The key to this passage lies in verse 29: God made man upright. This statement takes us back to the Garden of Eden and God's original design for the human race. This world is not right at present, Solomon says, but it's not God's fault. Men have gone in search of sensual pleasures and by following their base desires have strayed far from God. All of this is reminiscent of Isaiah 53:6, "We all, like sheep, have gone astray, each of us has turned to his own way."

Years ago I heard someone say that you shouldn't pray, "Lord, bless me," because sometimes we're simply not the kind of people God can bless. Sometimes—too often, I fear—we live self-centered lives and merely ask God to stamp His blessing on our personal agendas.

There is a better way to pray, and it goes like this: "Lord, please show me what You are blessing in the world so I can be a part of it." In essence, instead of asking God to adjust Himself to your will, you are saying, "Lord, show me what You are doing and let me be a part of it." Or to put it another way, instead of asking God to bless your agenda, you're asking God for the privilege of joining His agenda and making it your own.

There is truly a world of difference in those two prayers. Don't forget the principle: Find out what God is blessing and then go be a part of it.

Lord, I don't ask that You bless my agenda but that You show me Your agenda so that I may be blessed by doing the things that matter to You. Amen.

— ✳ —

SHINING THE LIGHT

✳ How many truly wise people do you know? What character qualities do they share?

✳ What is God blessing today? Are you a part of it?

— ✳ —

MORE LIGHT FROM GOD'S WORD
Read 1 Kings 11:1–3; Proverbs 31:10–31; and Titus 3:3–5.

※

Sixty-Three

THE RADIANT FACE

Who is like the wise man? Who knows the explanation of things? Wisdom brightens a man's face and changes its hard appearance.

Ecclesiastes 8:1

The face is the mirror of the soul. According to Exodus 34:29, Moses' face was radiant when he came down from Mount Sinai because he had seen the Lord. In Proverbs 15:13 Solomon also tells us that "a happy heart makes the face cheerful." Look at a person's face and you can discover a great deal about his or her walk with God.

Wisdom changes a person's face, making it beautiful to behold, according to Ecclesiastes 8:1. When I came to the church I now pastor, the Spurnys were one of the first families to befriend us. I don't know why that happened, but somehow we just became good friends. Every Sunday Mr. and Mrs. Spurny would come by, shake my hand, and Mrs. Spurny would smile at me. They taught me a little Czechoslovakian (a very little), and each week Mrs. Spurny would smile as I struggled to say a few words in her native tongue.

For several years before her death she struggled with cancer. Shortly before she died my associate pastor and I visited her at home. She looked so frail, so weak that we knew the end was not far away. Cancer had done its awful work. Despite her illness, she was as gracious as ever. As we sat at her kitchen table, my associate pastor read Psalm 34.

When he read verse 5, he stopped for a moment. "Those who look to him are radiant; their faces are never covered with shame." For some reason I had never noticed that particular verse. But when he read it, I looked at Mrs. Spurny. Her face was radiant. Although the cancer was taking her life, it had not destroyed her spirit. She said to us, "I'm not afraid to die. I'm ready to meet the Lord."

In heaven there is no more cancer, no more sickness, no more Alzheimer's disease, no more AIDS. In heaven there is only the radiance and joy of seeing Jesus Christ face-to-face.

That's the bottom line, isn't it? It is possible to face even the worst that life has to offer, and to face it with hope and optimism because the promises of God go beyond the grave.

Lord God, may the beauty of Jesus be seen in me. Amen.

— ✳ —

SHINING THE LIGHT

✳ Whose face comes to mind when you think of being radiant with the joy of the Lord? What do others see when they look at you?

✳ Take a quick look in the mirror. What do you see?

— ✳ —

MORE LIGHT FROM GOD'S WORD

Read Proverbs 24:5; Daniel 2:28–30; and Acts 6:8–15.

Sixty-Four

---*---

OBEY THE KING!

Obey the king's command, I say, because you took an oath before God. Do not be in a hurry to leave the king's presence. Do not stand up for a bad cause, for he will do whatever he pleases. Since a king's word is supreme, who can say to him, "What are you doing?" Whoever obeys his command will come to no harm, and the wise heart will know the proper time and procedure.

Ecclesiastes 8:2–5

Verses 2–5 offer practical, commonsense advice about loyalty and allegiance. Specifically, the oath in verse 2 refers to a vow of allegiance to obey a king. But it has many modern applications for those of us who have no king to obey. It certainly applies to employees who pick up a paycheck every two weeks. Whose signature is at the bottom? Who is paying your salary? You owe that person—or that company—your loyalty.

What if you feel that you can't obey his or her orders? Then quit and find a job compatible with your values. If you want to criticize, leave the company and then criticize to your heart's content. But don't sit in the "peanut gallery," making cheap comments about your superiors. That's just plain wrong. It's also stupid and will probably cost you your job eventually.

Does this mean we should never complain? No, not at all. But it does mean that we must recognize that "the authorities that exist have been established by God" (Romans 13:1). An authority is anyone who has the right to do something. If your job gives you the right to make certain decisions, then when you are on the job, you are an "authority." Seen in another light, an authority is anyone who has the right to make decisions that directly affect your life. In the broadest sense, all of us live in two relationships at once. We both have authority in certain areas and we are under authority in other areas. You may be a husband and thus the head of your home, but at work you are under the authority of your boss. You may be a teacher and thus the authority in your classroom, but you are under the authority of your principal, who is also under the authority of the school board. You may work in an office where certain people report to you while at the same time you report to someone over you. You are thus "in authority" and "under authority" at the same time.

You cannot be a leader until you know how to obey, and you cannot obey until you submit yourself to the authorities over you. This won't always be easy or convenient, and sometimes it can be very costly indeed. Solomon's advice is quite clear. Obey the king! Learn to obey, because someday you may be the one giving the orders.

Lord of all things, I pray for the grace to obey. Quell the rebel spirit within my heart. Amen.

207

—✳—

SHINING THE LIGHT

✳ Who are the "kings" in authority over you? In what
ways are you in authority over others?

✳ Where do you sense the rebel spirit in your own heart?

—✳—

MORE LIGHT FROM GOD'S WORD

Read 1 Chronicles 29:23–25; Proverbs 14:29; and
1 Peter 3:12–15.

✸

Sixty-Five

ONE THING I KNOW

For there is a proper time and procedure for every matter, though a man's misery weighs heavily upon him. Since no man knows the future, who can tell him what is to come? No man has power over the wind to contain it; so no one has power over the day of his death. As no one is discharged in time of war, so wickedness will not release those who practice it.

Ecclesiastes 8:6–8

Several weeks ago a friend received the news that his cancer is inoperable. The situation isn't hopeless, but that word *inoperable* somehow takes one's breath away. We live in a world of such amazing medical technology that we're surprised to hear that there are still some things the doctors can't cure with surgery.

What do you do in a moment like that? My friend is taking some pills as a form of chemotherapy. Perhaps the medicine will push back the cancer completely or buy him some time. Who knows? The doctors didn't make any promises, and even if they did, doctors aren't infallible. Another friend told me yesterday about his physician who always talks in percentages. But of course. What else does a doctor have but percentages and estimates based on past experience?

No one knows the future except God. We make educated guesses, which are sometimes right and sometimes wrong. The best and brightest among us must bow before the mysteries of the universe. As I look back over the last year, some things have happened that simply baffle the mind. I didn't see them coming, they surprised me when they got here, and I couldn't explain them afterwards.

Still we cry out for answers. "Why me? Why now? Why this?"

As I read the Book of Job, I am struck by the fact that no matter how many times he asked God for an explanation, Job never got one. So far as we know, Job never learned the real reason why he lost his children, his flocks, his crops, his health, and his home. In the end Job is humbled under the hand of a God whose ways are so mysterious and whose power so great that no human could ever understand Him, much less argue with Him.

There are some things we know and some things we don't know. I don't know why my friend has cancer. Even though I fervently pray for healing, I leave the future in the hands of a loving God. But there is one thing I know, and my friend knows it too, and Job knew it before either of us. I know that my Redeemer lives (Job 19:25). If you only know one thing, hang on to that truth and you'll be smiling all day long.

Give me a large supply of the Spirit of Christ, that I might submit in every trial and be at peace amid my uncertainties. Amen.

210

— ✳ —

SHINING THE LIGHT

* Do you believe that God is in control of everything that happens to you? Would this include both the good and bad experiences of life?

* Can anything happen to you that is not somehow part of God's plan for you?

— ✳ —

MORE LIGHT FROM GOD'S WORD

Read Isaiah 3:10–14; Luke 17:26–30; and Hebrews 3:7–11.

※

Sixty-Six

PRAYING FOR YOUR ENEMIES

All this I saw, as I applied my mind to everything done under the sun. There is a time when a man lords it over others to his own hurt. Then too, I saw the wicked buried—those who used to come and go from the holy place and receive praise in the city where they did this. This too is meaningless.
Ecclesiastes 8:9–10

I suppose one of the hardest commands in the Bible to obey is the command of Jesus that we should pray for our enemies. It is hard because prayer is the last thing we want to do for our enemies. Mostly, there are a lot of things we would like to do *to* our enemies.

I found some unexpected help in this area from the Book of Jeremiah. The background is this: King Nebuchadnezzar of Babylon had attacked Jerusalem and sent many of the people into exile. It was a humiliating experience for the people of God.

Not all of the Jews were taken to Babylon. Jeremiah was one of those who were left behind. He records a letter he sent from Jerusalem to the exiles in Babylon in order to encourage them. His words contain this message from the Lord: "Seek the peace and prosperity of the city to which I have carried you into exile. Pray to the Lord for it, because if it prospers, you too will prosper" (Jeremiah

29:7). God's Word is very simple: I put you in Babylon for a purpose. Although I know you are humiliated, discouraged, and angry, do not despair. And pray for the prosperity of Babylon.

Read that last phrase of verse 7 very carefully: "If it prospers, you too will prosper."

Many who read these words find themselves caught in a bad situation at work, or at school, or at home. Someone has hurt you deeply, and it's all you can do not to strike back. With all your energy, you barely hold back the bitterness. And some of it sloshes over the top now and then. You couldn't pray for your enemies if your life depended on it. But God says to do it anyway. That's the whole point of Jeremiah 29.

Every time we are faced with people who mistreat us, we have three options: 1. We can hate them with total hatred; that accomplishes nothing. 2. We can struggle to hold back our anger; that will emotionally exhaust us. 3. We can pray for God to bless them; that opens the door for God to bless us as well.

So here's a new reason to pray for your enemies. Your blessing depends on their prosperity.

Father, thank You for making my enemies a channel of blessing to me. Amen.

—✳—
SHINING THE LIGHT

✳ Who are your "enemies"?

✳ Have you prayed for those enemies recently? Did you
pray for them or against them?

—✳—
MORE LIGHT FROM GOD'S WORD
Read Genesis 39:1–5; Matthew 5:43–48; and Romans 12:17–21.

Sixty-Seven

---✴---

SLOW JUSTICE

When the sentence for a crime is not quickly carried out, the hearts of the people are filled with schemes to do wrong.

Ecclesiastes 8:11

The evening news had reported that a convicted killer on death row faces execution in just a few days. And now, on a network TV newsmagazine program, the face of a well-known minister fills the screen; he explains that this particular prisoner should not die by lethal injection. The minister is a longtime proponent of the death penalty—both on biblical and practical grounds. He believes that some crimes are so heinous that death is society's only proper response. In this case, however, he is willing to make an exception.

The Lord spoke to him, the minister says, and "laid it on my heart that I should pray" for this particular person. He has done that, he explains, and now favors commuting the sentence to life in prison without possibility of parole. The prisoner's life has been so radically changed by the gospel, he says, that execution would serve no purpose.

Then another face fills the screen. I do not recognize her but the text at the bottom calls her a "victim's rights advocate," which means she speaks on behalf of the family members who lost a loved one in a brutal murder fifteen years ago. She doesn't make the biblical argument; she simply notes that religious conversion of any kind should not be used as a reason to escape the death penalty. The law in this case is clear. The prisoner must die at the appointed hour.

Finally, a third face appears—the woman who hosts the show. She asks the preacher, "How can justice be served when the crime itself was committed fifteen years ago, and the case has taken years to come to trial, with the scheduled execution many years after that?"

The preacher has no quick reply, and indeed there's no easy answer to such a question. But it is "precisely on point," as lawyers like to say. Justice delayed is justice denied. Wrongdoers must be punished, and, in general, the quicker the better.

Solomon reminds us that evildoers take heart when the sentence is not quickly carried out. They interpret delay of judgment as meaning that judgment will never come. On a broad scale, this is one of the major objections made by nonbelievers against God. They mistake His forbearance for indifference, and thus they make an eternal mistake. Hell will be filled with people who thought they would never go there.

Lord God, may I never use Your patience as an excuse to sin. Amen.

— ✳ —

SHINING THE LIGHT

✳ Do you believe that it takes too long for lawbreakers to be sentenced for their crimes? If so, what should be done about it?

✳ Suppose that God punished you quickly for every sin you committed. What effect would that have on your life?

— ✳ —

MORE LIGHT FROM GOD'S WORD

Read Job 21:7–15; Psalm 10:1–11; and 2 Peter 3:3–10.

Sixty-Eight

IS GOD INTOLERANT?

Although a wicked man commits a hundred crimes and still lives a long time, I know that it will go better with God-fearing men, who are reverent before God. Yet because the wicked do not fear God, it will not go well with them, and their days will not lengthen like a shadow.

Ecclesiastes 8:12–13

We live in a "postmodern" age. If that term is new to you, it simply means that we live in an age in which our culture has largely abandoned the notion of truth. One hundred years ago most people shared a common moral code based to a large degree on the teachings of the Bible. Even people who were not Christian made their moral judgments based largely on what we today call the "Judeo-Christian" tradition. There was a large consensus that certain things were right and others wrong, that some things were permitted in society and others were not. That shared consensus gave enormous stability to the culture and allowed people from diverse backgrounds to live together in peace.

That consensus has almost entirely disappeared, which is why we can't decide how we feel about abortion, pornography, adultery, divorce, and gay (homosexual) rights. In the old days we didn't debate those issues because our shared value system taught us that it is wrong to kill unborn babies, that adultery is always evil, that homosexuality is shameful, and that pornography corrupts public morality. Today there is simply no widespread agreement on those issues. If the old Trinity was Father, Son, and Holy Spirit, the new trinity is tolerance, diversity, and pluralism. "All truth is relative." We worship tolerance, we celebrate diversity, and we praise pluralism. And woe to the man or woman who dares to speak against the new trinity.

One writer expressed the new view this way: "God, it seems to me, almost certainly is more intolerant of intolerance than of homosexuality, because intolerance is a greater violation of love, which by my reading of the Scriptures is the behavior God most desires in us."

Consider the assertion that God is "intolerant of intolerance." On the face of it, this appears to be a nonsensical statement. Nowhere in the Bible are we told that God is "intolerant of intolerance." Come to think of it, I'm not aware of any major Protestant, Catholic, or Orthodox creed that makes such a statement. To be "intolerant of intolerance" is an expression that has no real roots in classical theology of any kind.

Who are those who do not fear God? Those who do not fear, or respect, God are those who excuse sin and tolerate behavior that God calls evil. Solomon warns that in the end it will not go well for them. The debate over morality is as old as the human race because it goes back to the question the serpent asked Eve in the Garden of

Eden: "Has God indeed spoken?" The answer is yes, He has, and He has not stuttered. We would all be better off if we took His Word seriously.

O Lord, help me to stand on Your Word without fear, without favor, without compromise. Amen.

— ✳ —

SHINING THE LIGHT

✳ What evidence do you see to suggest that it will go better for God-fearing people than for the wicked?

✳ Describe a person who fears the Lord and one who doesn't. How does this difference play out in the crucial moral issues of this generation?

— ✳ —

MORE LIGHT FROM GOD'S WORD

Read 1 Kings 22:29–38; Psalm 112; and Matthew 13:47–50.

✳

Sixty-Nine

A TOPSY-TURVY WORLD

There is something else meaningless that occurs on earth: righteous men who get what the wicked deserve, and wicked men who get what the righteous deserve. This too, I say, is meaningless. So I commend the enjoyment of life, because nothing is better for a man under the sun than to eat and drink and be glad. Then joy will accompany him in his work all the days of the life God has given him under the sun.

Ecclesiastes 8:14–15

Life is filled with many mysteries. For instance, a tornado touches down on a quiet residential street. Fifteen seconds later twelve homes have been reduced to rubble. But it wasn't twelve homes in a row. It was four destroyed, then three skipped, then five gone, then one skipped, then three more hit.

How do you explain it? Should we assume that the twelve homes were destroyed because the people who lived in them deserved special punishment? What does that say about the residents of the four homes that were left untouched?

But we can ask the question another way. Why do murderers live forever while the good die young? "That's not true," you object. "Many murderers spend years in prison and some are put to death. And surely many good and decent people live to a ripe old age and die with their children and grandchildren gathered round them." I grant the point—and so does Solomon—that not all the wicked prosper, nor are all the righteous unfairly punished. But in a perfect world the wicked would never prosper and the righteous would never be punished. If the truth be told, there are enough criminals who seem to prosper that it does give a thoughtful person reason to pause.

Solomon's advice concerning this seeming injustice is simple. Don't worry about it. That's right, just don't worry about how God administers the universe. This may seem like cavalier or even cruel advice, but I think it means that we shouldn't worry about those things over which we have no control. I have a friend who uses a phrase that makes enormous sense at this point: "Feel free to have no opinion about that." What a liberating thought that is. Since you don't know why certain things happen, and since you can't figure it out by investigation, why worry about it?

Don't let your frustration with the big picture keep you from enjoying the present moment. Life is hard enough without taking on extra burdens you weren't meant to bear. Let God be God. In the meantime, enjoy the life He has given you. Feel free to have no opinion about how God runs the universe. Then go out and take on the day.

Sovereign Lord, I'm going to let You take care of Your business, and I ask You to help me take care of mine. Amen.

—✳—

SHINING THE LIGHT

✳ Can you think of anything that bothers you that you would be better off having no opinion about?

✳ Are you willing to trust God to run the universe without any input from you?

—✳—

MORE LIGHT FROM GOD'S WORD

Read Luke 23:13–25; Philemon 8–21; and 2 Thessalonians 1:5–10.

*

Seventy

LOOKING FOR ANSWERS

When I applied my mind to know wisdom and to observe man's labor on earth—his eyes not seeing sleep day or night—then I saw all that God has done. No one can comprehend what goes on under the sun. Despite all his efforts to search it out, man cannot discover its meaning. Even if a wise man claims he knows, he cannot really comprehend it.
Ecclesiastes 8:16–17

God's ways and ours are quite different. In verses 16–17 Solomon reminds us of that fundamental truth, writing that even if a man stays up all night he still won't fathom all that God has done. Nor can it be discovered by the application of human wisdom. What God does stands in a completely different category beyond our reach.

We see this clearly when we consider our spiritual salvation: It is by grace, wholly apart from human works. Everything within us fights against the notion that we contribute nothing to our own salvation. How, then, are we saved from God's wrath? If it is not by our own good works, how will we ever get to heaven? If not by our righteousness, then where will we find the righteousness we need?

One term coined during the Reformation nicely answers that question. John Calvin and Martin Luther said that we are saved by the application of an "alien righteousness." The word *alien* conjures up visions of strange little creatures with no hair and bulging eyes. But that's not what Luther and Calvin meant at all.

The term *alien* simply means "from another place." To say that we are saved by an "alien righteousness" means that we are saved by righteousness that comes "from another place." It comes not from within us as a result of our good deeds, but from outside of us entirely. Where, oh where, can a guilty sinner find righteousness "from another place"? He can find it in Jesus Christ! That's the "alien righteousness" that saves guilty sinners.

To make myself clear, I am saying that salvation is completely outside you and me. We do not save ourselves, and we contribute nothing to our salvation—nothing at all. God calls us, His Spirit draws, He gives us faith to believe, and He applies to us righteousness "from another place"—the righteousness of His Son, Jesus Christ.

This means there is nothing you can do to add to the work of Christ. It stands complete on its own. You either accept it or reject it—there is nothing in between.

Lord Jesus, thank You for providing righteousness from another place when I had nothing to offer but my own sins. Amen.

—✳—

SHINING THE LIGHT

✳ Why can't good works save us or help to save us?

✳ What does the term "alien righteousness" mean? Why must salvation come from someplace outside ourselves?

—✳—

MORE LIGHT FROM GOD'S WORD

Read Psalm 73; John 18:37; and 2 Corinthians 5:18–21.

Seventy-One

--- ✳ ---

MY LIFE IN GOD'S HANDS

*So I reflected on all this and concluded that the righteous
and the wise and what they do are in God's hands, but no
man knows whether love or hate awaits him. All share a
common destiny—the righteous and the wicked, the good
and the bad, the clean and the unclean, those who offer sac-
rifices and those who do not. As it is with the good man, so
with the sinner; as it is with those who take oaths, so with
those who are afraid to take them. This is the evil in everything that happens under the sun: The same destiny overtakes all. The hearts of men, moreover, are full of evil and
there is madness in their hearts while they live, and afterward they join the dead.*

Ecclesiastes 9:1–3

No man knows whether love or hate awaits him,"
Solomon declares in a short but telling phrase in
verse 1 of this passage. Here is the great mystery of death.
Seen from this side of the great divide, no one can say
with certainty what happens when we die.

We all wonder about life after death, don't we? It's
natural to think about it because sooner or later we're all
going to die. I was asked recently to pray for two elderly
women in our church, both facing the spectre of death.
One is over ninety and needs surgery but probably

wouldn't survive it; the other, age seventy-eight, is fighting pancreatic cancer. Both know Jesus Christ and are not afraid to die. When the staff and I met to pray, I told them we should ask that the Lord would let them die soon.

Many people would regard such a prayer as incredible. How can you pray that someone would die? You can pray that way only if you know for certain what will happen next, that there is lasting life after this earthly life. Some people try to peer behind the veil of death by reading about "near-death experiences."

A recent article reports that as many as 15 million Americans have had near-death experiences. Close to death, they had the sensation of leaving earth, or at least their body, and had a preview of "life on the other side." Some of them say they saw heaven. Many were changed forever by the things they experienced. They had touched eternity, or so they believed, and life on this earth could never be the same again.

In some ways, you can't blame the people of the world for looking to near-death experiences to answer their questions about life after death. If you don't know Jesus, you'll grasp at any straw. But if you know Him, you don't need to worry about those things. We don't need the word of people who nearly died when we have the word of someone who died on Friday and then came back to life on Sunday morning. He can be trusted when He said, "I am the resurrection and the life" (John 11:25).

What Solomon wrote is true as far as it goes. Everyone dies eventually. The grave is our common destiny. But is that the end? Or is there something more?

A friend told me about the last moments of his wife's life. As he held her in his arms, she took a few short breaths and then was gone. "I held her in my arms until Jesus came and took her in His arms," he said.

One of the verses of an old gospel song called "Since Jesus Came Into My Heart." contains this phrase: "There's a light in the valley of death now for me, since Jesus came into my heart." That light is the light of Jesus who came to be the light of the world. His light will shine a path for His people as they make the journey from earth to heaven.

Lord Jesus, what would we do with You? Where could we go but to the Lord? You alone have the words of eternal life. Thank You for hope that goes beyond the grave. Amen.

— ✳ —

SHINING THE LIGHT

✳ If you knew you were going to die tomorrow, how would you spend the next twenty-four hours?

✳ What destiny awaits you when you die?

— ✳ —

MORE LIGHT FROM GOD'S WORD

Read Psalm 116:15; John 5:28–29; and Zephaniah 2: 8–11.

✳

Seventy-Two

IF I SHOULD DIE
BEFORE I WAKE

Anyone who is among the living has hope—even a live dog is better off than a dead lion! For the living know that they will die, but the dead know nothing; they have no further reward, and even the memory of them is forgotten. Their love, their hate and their jealousy have long since vanished; never again will they have a part in anything that happens under the sun.

Ecclesiastes 9:4–6

I find enormous encouragement—and not a little humor—in the thought that a living dog is better than a dead lion (v. 4). A dead lion may be magnificent—but he is dead. Meanwhile that little yapping dog is still running in the front yard.

It's better to be alive than dead. This is what Solomon wants us to know. The dead see nothing, feel nothing, hear nothing, say nothing, and do nothing. They have vanished from the earth, never to return until they stand before God in judgment.

What if I knew how many days I had left on this earth? What difference would it make to me?

I wouldn't waste so much time on trivial things.

I would set two or three goals and work like crazy to see them accomplished.

I wouldn't get angry so easily or hold a grudge so long.

I would take time to hug my boys at least once a day.

I wouldn't spend so much time watching television.

I would say, "I love you" more often than I do.

I wouldn't complain about spinach or tuna casserole or time spent window-shopping at the mall.

I would write more letters.

I wouldn't worry about most of the things that currently bother me.

I wouldn't let pressure build up in the relationships that matter the most to me.

I wouldn't get disappointed when other people let me down.

I wouldn't put off saying "thank you" to others.

There are a few other things I would do if I knew I'd be here only a few months longer. I would:

- Be quick to ask forgiveness when I hurt someone.
- Pray every day for the love of Jesus to shine through my life.
- Spend more time with Marlene and my boys because soon enough my time with them will be over.
- Pray more, love more, laugh more, simplify my life, re-arrange my priorities, fret less, and concentrate on the things that really matter.

But if that's the way I would live, then why don't I live that way now? "We're all terminal," a friend reminded me. "Some of us just find out sooner than others."

Sovereign Lord, my life is in Your hands. May I not waste this day but use it fully to Your glory. Amen.

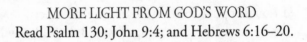

SHINING THE LIGHT

* What is the source of your hope? What worthwhile thing could you accomplish today with God's help?

* Name five ways your life would be different if you knew how many days you had left on earth.

MORE LIGHT FROM GOD'S WORD
Read Psalm 130; John 9:4; and Hebrews 6:16–20.

✳

Seventy-Three

HAVE A BLAST
WHILE YOU LAST

*Go, eat your food with gladness, and drink your wine with a
joyful heart, for it is now that God favors what you do. Always be clothed in white, and always anoint your head with
oil. Enjoy life with your wife, whom you love, all the days of
this meaningless life that God has given you under the sun—
all your meaningless days. For this is your lot in life and in
your toilsome labor under the sun. Whatever your hand finds
to do, do it with all your might, for in the grave, where you
are going, there is neither working nor planning nor knowledge nor wisdom.*

Ecclesiastes 9:7–10

My friend Shirley Banta likes to say, "Have a blast
while you last." That's what Solomon says in verses 7–10: We're not going to live forever, so we ought to
make the most of our life while we have the opportunity.
Life is not a dress rehearsal, so put your heart and soul
into it the first time around.

If your goal is to live a life of security and safety, one
warning: You'll end up with everything but Jesus. Our
Lord never took the safe road. He never took the easy
way. He never took a shortcut in order to play it safe. So
if that's what you're looking for, you might as well forget
about Jesus, because He doesn't have any part with that.

You can be old by the calendar and young at heart if you understand that the life of faith is inherently a life of risk. If you adopt that philosophy, you go through life full speed, with the throttle wide open, going for broke all the time.

May I share with you the goal of my life? I want to die young at a very old age. That's not just playing with words; that's a philosophy of life. Growing old is not just a matter of chronology. It's also a stage. You can be old at twenty and young at eighty-five. My goal is to die young at a very old age, doing everything I can for the cause of Christ.

I want to go down kicking and screaming and fighting and singing and laughing and playing and having a good time living my life till the day comes when they finally lower me into the ground.

The question is not "How old are you?" The question is "How old do you feel?"

How old was Abraham when his son Isaac was born? He was almost one hundred years old. How old was Moses when he led the Jews out of Egypt? He was eighty years old. Correction: He was eighty years young. An old man could never do what Moses did.

This chronology stuff is overrated. A life of faith can keep you active and young at heart. Looked at in that light, the statement "Have a blast while you last" is far more than a slogan. It's the most biblically based philosophy of life I've ever discovered.

Living by faith means that you live until you die and

you don't die until you're dead.

Lord, help me to squeeze every drop of joy out of life today. Amen.

—✳—

SHINING THE LIGHT

* List three reasons why you are glad to be alive right now.

* How old do you feel? If you were accused of enjoying life too much, would there be enough evidence to convict you?

—✳—

MORE LIGHT FROM GOD'S WORD

Read Song of Songs 7:1–13; Matthew 5:1–11; and Luke 6:46–49.

※

Seventy-Four

DAMON RUNYON'S REMARK

I have seen something else under the sun: The race is not to the swift or the battle to the strong, nor does food come to the wise or wealth to the brilliant or favor to the learned; but time and chance happen to them all.

Ecclesiastes 9:11

Damon Runyon was a famous New York columnist in the first half of the twentieth century. He once offered this wry observation on our text: "The race is not to the swift or the battle to the strong, but that's the way to bet." Solomon wouldn't disagree at all. He would merely point out that the swift don't always come in first, nor do the strong win every battle. You win some, you lose some. That's life.

I read recently about a pastor who has the following sign hanging in his office:

Walt, Do not feel totally, personally,
irrevocably responsible for everything.
That's My job! Love, God!

In the movie *Rudy*, a college student hopes yet despairs of making the Notre Dame football team. The title character is too small, too slow, too weak, and in every way fails to meet the challenge. Totally discouraged,

Rudy goes to a priest and asks if he will ever make the team. The priest smiles and says that in thirty-five years he has learned only two things for certain: "First, there is a God, and second, I'm not Him."

Yes, God is in control, often in ways we cannot understand or even imagine, yet always in good, wise ways. Consider the birth of Christ—the central miracle of the Christian faith. Theologians call this the incarnation— which means to take the form of human flesh. Skeptics and unbelievers have attacked our faith at precisely this point—the "silly" notion that God could ever become a man, much less a baby.

But that is precisely what happened at Bethlehem. Either you believe that or you don't. If you don't, then all the miracles of the Bible will seem impossible to you. But if you do believe that, then you shouldn't have trouble believing anything else the Bible says. You will be able to believe an all-powerful God can bring all things to pass.

Many Christians struggle with a heavy load of worries about the future. There are career questions, health issues, family problems, financial difficulties, and a host of unfulfilled dreams. We wonder if the future will simply mean more of the same. Sometimes we truly feel that everything depends on us and that we are "totally, personally, irrevocably responsible for everything." When that happens, we should ponder the miracle of Christmas.

Ponder, for instance, these miracles of Christmas: God can arrange for a virgin to become pregnant. He can cause a Roman ruler to order a census at precisely the right moment in history. He can ensure that the baby will be born at exactly the place prophesied seven hundred years earlier. He can bring together angels, shepherds, and wise men to celebrate that miraculous birth. And He can take a tiny baby born in a stable and make that baby the Savior of the world.

Now if God can do all that, what are you so worried about?

God of the impossible, may I never doubt Your power or believe that You are not equal to my circumstances. Amen.

———✳———

SHINING THE LIGHT

✳ Do you agree with Damon Runyon's remark? Why or why not?

✳ What does this teach us about making our own plans for the future?

———✳———

MORE LIGHT FROM GOD'S WORD

Read Luke 2:1–20; Galatians 5:16–26; and James 4:13–17.

✳

Seventy-Five

LIKE FISH IN THE NET

Moreover, no man knows when his hour will come: As fish are caught in a cruel net, or birds are taken in a snare, so men are trapped by evil times that fall unexpectedly upon them.

Ecclesiastes 9:12

No person knows when his or her final hour will come. How often are we reminded of this solemn truth. Yesterday I received word that a distinguished minister in our own city died suddenly after an early morning prayer meeting. I knew him slightly and admired him from a distance. Over thirty years ago he had founded the church where he served as pastor until his death at age fifty-five. Not a heart attack, the doctors said, but a blood clot or an aneurysm. He preached last Sunday with no idea it was his last time in the pulpit. Here today, gone tomorrow.

Solomon uses two images from nature to drive home the unexpected nature of death. Fish swim serenely in the ocean, then suddenly they are scooped up in the net. Birds fly freely through the air, then stumble into a hidden snare. The whole point is that very few of us know the precise moment of our own death. For every person who lives to a ripe old age and dies surrounded by family and friends, there are many more who are struck down much earlier by a wasting disease or a disastrous accident.

One day you're feeling fine, the next you notice a lump in your neck or a strange pain in your ribs. Or you're driving down the road, absentmindedly flipping the stations on your radio when a truck jumps the median divider and hits your car head-on. Or you might be caught in a drive-by shooting. Who knows? The list of possible ways to die is endless.

Since you can't know the moment of your own death, the best you can do is to (1) accept that reality, and (2) be prepared when the moment comes. As a practical matter, that certainly involves having your will up-to-date, keeping short accounts with God and with others, and making sure that the people you love the most know how much you love them.

On another level, it means following Martin Luther's advice. The father of the Reformation said that a man should always live with the day of his death on his mind. Perhaps in modern management terms that means beginning with the end in view.

You won't live forever. You may not see another sunrise. You may find yourself unexpectedly dead in the next twenty-four hours. Here is some wise advice: Live each day as though it were your last—and one day you'll be right.

Gracious God, since nothing can befall me today without Your express permission, help me to live with excitement and not with fear. Amen.

— ✴ —

SHINING THE LIGHT

✴ Can you think of an instance where death came suddenly to someone you knew personally?

✴ What steps have you taken to prepare for your own death? What would you say is the "unfinished business" of your life at this point?

— ✴ —

MORE LIGHT FROM GOD'S WORD

Read Nahum 1:2–7; Acts 12:20–25; and Hebrews 2:14–15.

※

Seventy-Six

THE PARABLE OF THE SMALL CITY

I also saw under the sun this example of wisdom that greatly impressed me: There was once a small city with only a few people in it. And a powerful king came against it, surrounded it and built huge siegeworks against it. Now there lived in that city a man poor but wise, and he saved the city by his wisdom. But nobody remembered that poor man. So I said, "Wisdom is better than strength." But the poor man's wisdom is despised, and his words are no longer heeded.

Ecclesiastes 9:13–16

Does the treatment of the poor man in Ecclesiastes 9: 13–16 surprise you? Today he probably would be hailed as a hero. We would praise the poor man for his ingenuity in saving the city from defeat at the hands of an overwhelming force. We aren't told how he did it—and perhaps the details don't matter. Certainly it was some combination of skill, tenacity, surprise, and perhaps a bit of derring-do that saved the day.

The man does deserve great praise. A ticker-tape parade would not be out of order. In today's world we would certainly name a high school after him along with a boulevard and perhaps a major airport. No doubt he would appear on all the morning news shows, and his life story would be told on a special one-hour biography. It's not hard to imagine that he would receive enough job offers to guarantee that he would never be poor again.

But that's not what happened. Artist Andy Warhol remarked that in the future everyone would get their fifteen minutes of fame and then be forgotten. Certainly we live in a culture of instant gratification where the central question is, "What have you done for me lately?" So after the first round of interviews the poor man is never heard from again. "Hey, let us know when you save another city and we'll be glad to do another interview." So maybe the ultimate treatment of the poor man isn't so surprising after all. That's the way of the world—which makes this story so believable.

We can moan and groan about it but Solomon would say, "Stop whining. The world forgets its heroes." If you're waiting for someone to thank you for doing a good deed, you might have to wait a long time. Doing good is its own reward. And if you do your deeds to be seen by men, you'll have your reward and nothing else to show for it (Matthew 6:1–4). If you do good simply because you have a chance to do it, you might or might not be rewarded on earth, but you will not be forgotten in heaven. This is the promise of Jesus.

As Solomon has reminded us many times, the world is a cruel place, sometimes rewarding the bad guys and punishing the good ones. More often the good guys are simply forgotten. Better days are coming, but they're not here yet.

Holy Lord, help me to remember that though the good I do today may be quickly forgotten on earth, it will be remembered forever in heaven. Amen.

—✳—

SHINING THE LIGHT

✳ Why are we so quick to forget the good that others do on our behalf? How do you respond when others fail to appreciate what you do for them?

✳ Name three people who deserve a "thank you" from you today.

—✳—

MORE LIGHT FROM GOD'S WORD

Read 2 Samuel 9:1–13; Matthew 6:1–4; and Luke 17:11–19.

Seventy-Seven

✳

QUIET WORDS
OF THE WISE

The quiet words of the wise are more to be heeded than the shouts of a ruler of fools. Wisdom is better than weapons of war, but one sinner destroys much good.

Ecclesiastes 9:17–18

It had been a "jumpy" kind of day. I got up a little earlier than usual because I had so much to do. I piled some books in my car and left for church, hoping to do two days' work in one. By 11:00 A.M. I was frazzled. Nothing had gone particularly wrong, but nothing had gone especially right either. And I had two afternoon appointments, a church meeting that night, and another appointment after that. It was just going to be one of those frustrating days that you just plow through with your head buried in your work.

So I went downstairs to pick up my mail. Among the clutter of newspapers and junk mail was a letter from a friend. I didn't open it at first because . . . well, because I was frazzled and who needs trouble when you feel frazzled?

But when I opened it, the letter wasn't that way at all. My friend began by writing, "You are always so busy greeting parishioners and visitors after the morning service that I am reluctant to say 'Hi!'" He went on to thank me for a recent sermon and to comment on how he was trying to apply it in his own life.

Then he added a word about a mutual friend, whose wife recently died. He even sent along a copy of a nice letter that our friend had written, thanking him for his letter of condolence.

There followed two paragraphs of encouragement concerning specific areas of our church life. The letter ended with a simple line: "Ray, keep the faith and your thoughtful leadership going!"

That was all. Just a nice letter of encouragement from a friend. But the Lord arranged it so that I would receive it on a day when I felt more frazzled than thoughtful.

When I put the letter down, a smile broke across my face and I felt relaxed for the first time all day. My frazzle quotient dropped by 75 percent.

Solomon reminds us that "an anxious heart weighs a man down, but a kind word cheers him up" (Proverbs 12:25). Commentator Robert Alden notes, "Today doctors are just beginning to estimate the terrible effects stress has on the physical body, yet look at the same truth expressed in this ancient book!" Another writer said, "Who has not in himself had this experience, how such a word of friendly encouragement from a sympathizing heart cheers the sorrowful soul, and, if only for a time, changes its sorrow into the joy of confidence and of hope!"

My friend's letter did all that and more. Frazzle was down, stress was down, worry was down; joy was up, peace was up, good cheer was up. All that, and it wasn't even noon yet!

It's amazing how much good you can do with a few words of encouragement.

My Father, I pray for the gift of being a load-lifter today. Amen.

——✳——

SHINING THE LIGHT

✳ What person comes to your mind when you think of the phrase "quiet words of the wise"? Would anyone think of you in that regard?

✳ Ask God to use you as a "load-lifter" this week.

——✳——

MORE LIGHT FROM GOD'S WORD

Read Proverbs 18:21; Ephesians 4:29; and Colossians 3:8.

※

Seventy-Eight

DEAD FLIES IN
THE OLD SPICE

As dead flies give perfume a bad smell, so a little folly out-weighs wisdom and honor. The heart of the wise inclines to the right, but the heart of the fool to the left. Even as he walks along the road, the fool lacks sense and shows everyone how stupid he is.

Ecclesiastes 10:1–3

It isn't often that our house is plunged into crisis, but it happened just the other day when our refrigerator stopped working. Or to be more precise, when our refrigerator stopped keeping things cold. It was still working in the sense that the motor was humming and the light came on when you opened the door. But soon our ice melted into a pool of water, and all our frozen food slowly turned to yucky mush.

Time to call the repairman. We found a coupon offering $25 off any service call, made an appointment, and within several hours a friendly man arrived on our doorstep. He fiddled with this dial and that gizmo for a couple of minutes. Then he made a solemn announcement, "I think we may have a little friend caught in the fan." What little friend might that be? Sometimes a mouse will smell food and then get tangled in the condenser fan. End of mouse and end of cold air.

Sure enough, he was right. When he removed the bottom panel, there was our little friend, contorted upon the blades of death. Within ten minutes he had replaced the fan and was on his way. The bill came to just over $200.

As Solomon has noted, it doesn't take many flies to make the perfume stink. And it takes only a little rodent to make a big refrigerator fail. Similarly, a little sin can cause enormous damage.

Have you heard of Peter Jenkins? He's the man who walked across America. When he had finished his trip, someone asked him if he ever felt like quitting. He said yes, he felt that way many times. What was it that made him feel like quitting? The high mountains? The searing sun? The lonely nights? The possibility of danger? No, none of that. It was the sand in his shoes. It's not the big things that hurt us spiritually. It's the little things—the sand in the shoes—that we neglect to take care of.

Little things become big, irritations become annoyances, and annoyances become sore spots. Over time sore spots become open wounds of bitterness. The infection spreads until it controls your whole life.

These things happen because we let the sand stay in our shoes. Little molehills of frustration not dealt with soon become big mountains of bitterness. Make it a priority to deal with the little things before those little things become big.

Loving Lord, protect me today from making some stupid mistake that will dishonor You, hurt others, and cause me to sin. May I live so that I will have nothing to regret when this day is done. Amen.

—✳—

SHINING THE LIGHT

✳ Can you think of a foolish mistake you made that ended up hurting you and others? Name several positive lessons you have learned from your mistakes.

✳ What is the greatest temptation you face right now?

—✳—

MORE LIGHT FROM GOD'S WORD

Read Numbers 32:23; Proverbs 28:13; and Ephesians 5:1–8.

Seventy-Nine

DEALING WITH
DIFFICULT PEOPLE

*If a ruler's anger rises against you, do not leave your post;
calmness can lay great errors to rest. There is an evil I have
seen under the sun, the sort of error that arises from a ruler:
Fools are put in many high positions, while the rich occupy
the low ones. I have seen slaves on horseback, while princes
go on foot like slaves.*

Ecclesiastes 10:4–7

A t the office, in the classroom, on the assembly line,
living next door, and sometimes sharing the same
bedroom are people who occasionally get on our nerves.
Perhaps that's putting it too mildly. There are some people we just can't stand. Marshall Shelley wrote about the
difficult people that pastors encounter, calling them
"well-intentioned dragons." I like that because it nicely
balances the reality most of us face every day.

We all have a few well-intentioned dragons around
us. That's a given. It's how we deal with them that matters.

I used to think that those hard-to-live-with people
were simply one more proof of universal depravity. In a
fallen world some people are going to look a bit more
"fallen" than the rest of us. That's certainly true, but as

the years pass, I've come to realize that God actually sends the dragons our way for a positive purpose. They are grace-builders, sent on a mission from God to make us better people. Without them, life would be easier but we would be spiritually flabby. Because of them, we are forced to grow in areas that would otherwise remain undeveloped for God.

There are four ways we commonly deal with difficult people:

1. We ignore them. We do this by shutting the door, leaving the room, hanging up the phone, or telling our secretary not to let Mr. Jones know we're in the office today.

2. We intimidate them. Intimidation works when the troublesome person happens to be a wife, a brother, a sister, or a child. Intimidators use violence and the threat of violence, harsh language, half-truths, body language, and a myriad of ugly facial expressions to keep people in line and get their own way.

3. We argue with them. I personally find this a major temptation since I love a good argument.

4. We destroy them. We do that through subtle means, such as attacking a person behind his back, passing along bits of gossip, leaking confidential information, reporting on the moral failures of those we despise, and implying that others may have done wrong when we have no proof. A friend once told me about one of his colleagues

who could "stick a knife in you and you wouldn't know it until you looked down and saw your blood on the floor."

Against all this we have the example of Jesus, who always spoke the truth with love. He never intimidated, never threatened, and never ignored difficult people. Follow His example and you can't go wrong.

Father, I pray for a teachable spirit today so that I might learn something from the difficult people in my life. Amen.

—✳—

SHINING THE LIGHT

✳ Have you ever worked under someone you considered a fool? What happened?

✳ Why is it crucial to keep your temper when your boss is angry at you? How should Christians respond when we find ourselves in an unfair situation at work?

—✳—

MORE LIGHT FROM GOD'S WORD
Read Daniel 6; Luke 12:1–12; and Ephesians 6:5–9.

Eighty

"THESE THINGS HAPPEN"

Whoever digs a pit may fall into it; whoever breaks through a wall may be bitten by a snake. Whoever quarries stones may be injured by them; whoever splits logs may be endangered by them.

Ecclesiastes 10:8–9

James Herriot, a British veterinarian and best-selling author, describes in one of his books the stoic philosophy of the farmers who live in the rugged Yorkshire Dells. When disease decimates a herd of sheep or a sudden storm ruins an entire harvest, the farmers take it in stride, often saying nothing more than "These things happen."

Such a statement may seem like fatalism to outsiders, but to those hardy farmers it represents a realistic appraisal of life. No matter how much one plans or how hard he works, he could lose it all to an apparently random act of nature.

It happens all the time. Faulty wiring causes a fire that burns down a building, wiping out a business and putting seventy-four people out of work. One man's life savings go up in flames—the work of thirty years lost in thirty minutes. Upon investigation it is discovered that the wiring has been faulty for years, which means that the blaze could have started at any time. Why now? And why didn't someone discover the problem sooner?

"These things happen." If we deny it, we simply deny reality itself. A wise person understands that the best business plan in the world is just that—a plan, a projection, an idea about what the future may hold. The only thing you can know for certain is that the future won't work out exactly the way you planned.

Most of us know about Murphy's Law: If anything can go wrong, it will. Perhaps you've also heard of Johnson's Comment: Murphy was an optimist. If you're planning to succeed in this fallen world, make sure you leave plenty of room for the possibility of failure, trouble, catastrophe, and sudden setbacks.

You might fall into a well. Or you might be bitten by a serpent. Or you might be cut by flying rocks. Or injured while you are splitting logs. Those Yorkshire farmers are right. "These things happen." The only way to avoid potential calamity is never to dig, never to build, never to chop; in short, to stay in bed all day watching TV. But you could be electrocuted in your bathroom or trip and break your leg in the kitchen.

There aren't any guarantees in life. Bad things sometimes happen to people in the middle of their normal work. Other people are standing around doing nothing when suddenly a flowerpot hits them on the head. The only solution is to do your job, accept the risks that go with it, take appropriate precautions, and understand that things could still go haywire.

Does that sound like a contradiction? It isn't. It's just plain common sense. Let's call it Solomon's Observation: Expect the worst and sooner or later you won't be disappointed. You don't have to be a pessimist to survive in the world, but starry-eyed optimists generally don't last very long either.

Spirit of God, I pray for the grace not to be overly surprised by anything that happens to me today. Amen.

—✳—

SHINING THE LIGHT

✳ What practical steps have you taken to be prepared for the "accidents" of life?

✳ Do you agree that we live in a Murphy's Law universe? How can we remain hopeful in the face of the unexpected problems we all face on a daily basis?

—✳—

MORE LIGHT FROM GOD'S WORD

Read Jonah 1; Romans 5:3–5; and 1 Corinthians 16:5–9.

Eighty-One

BE PREPARED

If the ax is dull and its edge unsharpened, more strength is needed but skill will bring success. If a snake bites before it is charmed, there is no profit for the charmer.

Ecclesiastes 10:10–11

Would Solomon have joined the Boy Scouts? I don't know, but I'm sure he would agree with their well-known motto: Be prepared. His two illustrations in verses 10–11 show the danger of approaching our work in a haphazard fashion.

First is the man whose job is splitting wood. Because he is too lazy to sharpen the ax, he has to work much harder than necessary. Sharpening an ax is a relatively simple job, taking at most only a few minutes at the beginning of the day. But perhaps this fellow is in a big hurry or maybe he didn't bother to check the blade or possibly he would rather spend those few minutes drinking coffee with his buddies. In any case, the blade remains dull; but the work has to be done, so he ends up straining his back from all the extra effort.

The case of the snake charmer is similar. Snake charming requires a certain degree of preparation and a large dose of good timing, or else the charmer's career will be a short one. When the snake bites too soon, the charmer loses the money he would have made. In today's world, he would probably have a lawsuit on his hands from a very unhappy customer.

There are many ways to apply these verses, but one of the most obvious has to do with taking the time to learn your craft thoroughly. To rise to the top in any profession requires a certain amount of skill plus a great deal of determination. The world is filled with talented men and women who never amount to much because they are unable (or unwilling) to pay the price to hone their God-given abilities.

The great temptation is to join the "good enough" club, as in "that's good enough for government work"—which is a slander on every dedicated public servant. The apostle Paul urges us to do our work "with sincerity of heart and reverence for the Lord" (Colossians 3:22), understanding that someday we will stand before Him and give an account for the quality of our daily work.

When God asked Moses, "What is that in your hand?" he replied, "A staff" (Exodus 4:2). That staff became the sign of God's miraculous power to deliver His people out of Egypt. What talent has God placed in your hand? Are you willing to offer it to Him?

Teacher of Truth, You have ordained that I should be a lifetime student in the classroom of life. May I not waste the lessons You are teaching me today. Amen.

— ✳ —

SHINING THE LIGHT

* What areas of your life need "sharpening" right now? What is the major task facing you in the next twenty-four hours?

* Name three life lessons you have learned in recent months.

— ✳ —

MORE LIGHT FROM GOD'S WORD
Read Ruth 3:1–14; Luke 1:37; and 2 Peter 3:18.

———— ✳ ————

Eighty-Two

FOOLS AND THEIR FOOLISH WORDS

Words from a wise man's mouth are gracious, but a fool is consumed by his own lips. At the beginning his words are folly; at the end they are wicked madness—and the fool multiplies words. No one knows what is coming—who can tell him what will happen after him? A fool's work wearies him; he does not know the way to town.

Ecclesiastes 10:12–15

Once again we are reminded that fools talk too much. When first we meet such a person, his unending chatter may seem pleasing to us. He laughs and jokes his way through life, pointing out the lighter side of even the saddest moments. He's a riot, the life of the party, a fun guy to have around. He's a cutup, and if you only see him now and then, he seems like a great person to know. But those who know him better don't share that high opinion. Humor is like rich spice: A little goes a long way, but too much spoils the meal.

What starts out as harmless folly ends up as wicked madness. Either he won't stop or perhaps he can't. Foolish words flow like a torrent out of his mouth. It's all there—flippant humor, coarse jesting, irreverent teasing, unkind insults, silly stories, inane comments—some of it funny but nearly all of it inappropriate.

A wise person once remarked that it's better to be thought a fool than to open your mouth and remove all doubt. Consider the benefits of silence: (1) You can listen carefully to what others say; (2) you have time to frame your thoughts; (3) your companions will value your words because you have listened to them; and (4) you run a much lower risk of saying something foolish.

If that last reason sounds too negative, consider Proverbs 10:19, "When words are many, sin is not absent, but he who holds his tongue is wise."

Spirit of God, I pray for the gift of sanctified brevity. Amen.

———✳———

SHINING THE LIGHT

✳ When are you most tempted to talk too much? What steps can you take to say less today?

✳ Pause and commit your lips to the Lord for His glory.

———✳———

MORE LIGHT FROM GOD'S WORD

Read Psalm 19:14; Proverbs 17:27–28; and James 3:2–12.

✳

Eighty-Three

LEADERS GOOD AND BAD

Woe to you, O land whose king was a servant and whose princes feast in the morning. Blessed are you, O land whose king is of noble birth and whose princes eat at a proper time—for strength and not for drunkenness.

Ecclesiastes 10:16–17

Warren Bennis is an educator, a philosopher, an author, a scholar, and a keen observer of the American scene. These are his words: "Leadership is a word that is on everyone's lips. The young fight against it. Police seek it. Experts claim it. The artists spurn it. Scholars want it. Bureaucrats pretend to have it and politicians wish they could find it. Everyone agrees on this one fact. There is less of it today than there used to be."

If I could add a footnote, it would be that we face a crisis of leadership inside the Christian church. Turn on the radio. Open the newspaper. Watch the 10 P.M. news for yet another story about a Catholic priest, a Protestant pastor, a vicar, a prelate, a spiritual leader caught in yet another moral failure, financial scandal, ecclesiastical upheaval—some shocking new revelation almost every week.

We are at that point in history where a generation of church leaders is passing from the scene. The leaders who rose to prominence after World War II are now retiring. Who will replace Billy Graham? Where will we find another theologian like Carl Henry? Who will be the next Francis Schaeffer to take the gospel and apply it to the problems of the modern world?

Solomon makes clear that we need leaders who will take their jobs seriously. They must be men and women who display the virtue of self-control. Leaders who party all day ("feast in the morning") bring nothing but sorrow to those who follow them. Leaders who eat at the proper time possess the forgotten virtue of self-control. Paul lists self-control in 1 Timothy 3:2 and Titus 1:8 as a nonoptional qualification for spiritual leaders. The word he uses literally means to have a "safe mind"—that is, one not clouded by emotional mood swings or by artificial stimulants. The self-controlled person is experienced enough to keep his balance when life throws him a curveball. The word *self-control* also implies a sober and serious attitude. The person is not a goof or a lightweight flake. He or she is serious about spiritual things. This individual is great to have around when a tough decision needs to be made because he doesn't jump to conclusions or act solely on the basis of his emotions. He knows the right thing to do and isn't afraid to do it.

Blessed are the leaders who have discovered the power to do what they ought to do. Blessed are they, and blessed are those who follow them.

O Lord, pour out Your grace upon our leaders. Fill them with wisdom and courage to follow in the paths of righteousness so that we might live in peace and our land be blessed by You. Amen.

— ✳ —

SHINING THE LIGHT

✳ Do you agree that leadership is a noble calling from the Lord?

✳ In your opinion what are the three most important qualities of a good leader? Why is character an all-important issue in leadership?

— ✳ —

MORE LIGHT FROM GOD'S WORD

Read Proverbs 28:12; Daniel 4; and 1 Timothy 3:1–8.

※

Eighty-Four

NO ROOM FOR SLUGGARDS

If a man is lazy, the rafters sag; if his hands are idle, the house leaks.

Ecclesiastes 10:18

Hard work is a Christian virtue. The call to hard work is a call to truly purposeful living. It means not wasting your life but rather doing something with the opportunities that God has placed before you. It means that instead of wasting your days as a couch potato, you decide to get up and get busy. So many Christians just while away the hours, looking at the flowers, consulting with the rain. The game of life is being played all around us, and we are sitting on the bench, sound asleep.

Though your work will differ from my work and from everybody else's work, the elements of success are always the same: planning, forethought, diligence, enthusiasm, and a full commitment to whatever God has called you to do.

Are your rafters sagging? Get up and do something about it. Does your roof leak? Get up and plug those holes.

There is a world out there. Get in it. Don't sit on the sidelines. God gave you two hands; use them. God gave you a voice; speak up. Get up and in the name of God do something. Use your power, your intelligence, your vision, your gifts, and all that God gave you to make the world a better place.

Here is the application. What is it that you know you need to do this week that is undone in your life? It will take you less than three seconds to answer that question. I already know what it is in my life. Now that you know what it is, name it. Plan it. Schedule it. Do it. Whatever your hand finds to do, do it with all your might because in the grave where you are going there is no planning, no foresight, no work. You want to rest? You will have plenty of time to rest after the grave. Until then, stay busy doing what needs to be done.

O God, help me to do my work as if Your reputation depended upon it. Amen.

—✳—

SHINING THE LIGHT

✳ Do you have a reputation as a hard worker? What would your friends say?

✳ How many unfinished projects are there in your life right now?

—✳—

MORE LIGHT FROM GOD'S WORD
Read Proverbs 24:30–34; 1 Thessalonians 1:3; and 2 Thessalonians 3:6–13.

※

Eighty-Five

WHAT MONEY CAN'T BUY

A feast is made for laughter, and wine makes life merry, but money is the answer for everything.

Ecclesiastes 10:19

The final phrase of verse 19 might have caught your attention: "Money is the answer for everything." Indeed, commentators differ on its meaning. Is this an ironic jab at those who think money can solve every problem, or is this Solomon's sober evaluation of life as it stands? I suggest the latter as more appropriate because in one sense money is indeed the answer for everything.

The Bible never condemns money per se. A quarter is a morally neutral object—capable of being spent in a million different ways—some good, some not so good, and some positively evil. That quarter can be combined with others to provide food for a homeless man; it can also purchase pornography; or it can make a phone call to a lonely grandmother. The coin could end up traveling to Thailand to buy a hymnbook, or it could help to pay the first installment on a semester's college tuition. A teenager could use it to help buy a blouse—or bullets for a street gang. Who knows? In each case the moral value of money is determined by the ends to which it is put.

Jesus made the same point in Luke 16:9: "I tell you,

use worldly wealth to gain friends for yourselves, so that when it is gone, you will be welcomed into eternal dwellings." Notice the reason He gives—"so that when it is gone." What is the "it" He is talking about? Money and everything money can buy. Money fails in the end. Five minutes after you are dead someone else will have your money. Five minutes after death your checkbook will be useless to you. Think of it. All you live for, the accumulated wealth of a lifetime, everything you dreamed about, every cent you ever saved, every investment—all of it is gone forever.

After a rich man dies, people often say, "How much did he leave?" The answer is always the same: He left it all. The question is not, How much did you make? The question is, How did you spend what you had while you had it? Did you buy houses, land, stocks, furniture, new cars, new clothes? Is that all you did with your money? Was that the goal of your life? Or did you use your money to invest in things that will last forever? Those are your only two choices.

Father, thank You for so many good gifts. I pray for the wisdom to enjoy all that is mine and to use it for Your glory. Amen.

—✳—

SHINING THE LIGHT
✳ In what sense is money the answer for everything?

✳ Name three things money can't buy. Name three worthwhile things you could do if you had enough money.

—✳—

MORE LIGHT FROM GOD'S WORD
Read Proverbs 8:10–19; Luke 12:27–34; and 1 Corinthians 3:10–15.

✳

Eighty-Six

LITTLE BIRDS ARE LISTENING

*Do not revile the king even in your thoughts, or curse the
rich in your bedroom, because a bird of the air may carry
your words, and a bird on the wing may report what you say.*
Ecclesiastes 10:20

The above verse wraps up a section that deals with
what we might call good citizenship. The Pulpit
Commentary groups verses 16–20 under the title "Duties
of rulers and subjects," with verses 16–19 dealing with
good and bad rulers and verse 20 covering the duty of
loyalty on the part of subjects.

Fundamentally verse 20 contains a warning against
too much loose talk. We could paraphrase it: "Be careful
what you say because your casual comments may get
back to those in authority and you could end up in big
trouble." Even a "harmless" joke around the office water-
cooler may sound much different when it is repeated in
your supervisor's office. We needn't assume that the person doing the speaking has mischief or malice in his
heart. He may, but that's not the point. Sometimes in a
moment of frustration we may blow off steam, saying
things we don't really mean, or at least saying things in
small pieces that we wouldn't say if given the chance to
state them in a thoughtful manner. Or we may make a

comment—humorous or not—that is truly innocent but somehow can be misinterpreted by others and used against us later. How many people have lost their jobs or any chance at career advancement precisely because they were judged to be loose cannons who could not be trusted?

Underlying this warning lies the truth that even bad leaders deserve our respect. If we believe in God at all, we must believe that promotion comes from the Lord (Psalm 75:5–6) and that the "powers that be" are ordained by God (Romans 13:1). He raises up one ruler and brings down another. This applies just as much to office politics as to national politics. Your boss is where he is because God wants him there—which means that sometimes unworthy people are promoted to places of authority for reasons known only to God.

The lesson is clear. Be careful what you say about those in authority over you. Loose lips sink ships. They can also sink your career. So watch what you say.

Lord God, set a seal upon my lips lest I should say anything in private that I would be embarrassed to hear repeated in public. Amen.

— ✳ —

SHINING THE LIGHT

✳ How would you feel if everything you said in the last forty-eight hours was broadcast over the radio? Would you have any reason to be embarrassed or ashamed?

* How do you spot a person whose lips are truly under God's control?

——✳——

MORE LIGHT FROM GOD'S WORD

Read Exodus 22:28; 2 Kings 2:23–25; and Acts 23:1–5.

※

Eighty-Seven

BREAD UPON THE WATERS

Cast your bread upon the waters, for after many days you will find it again. Give portions to seven, yes to eight, for you do not know what disaster may come upon the land.

Ecclesiastes 11:1–2

Several years ago I met Jack, a salesman who had changed careers when he was thirty-seven. I asked if it wasn't risky to leave his teaching position for the uncertain world of sales, especially since he had a wife and a young daughter to consider.

"Yes, it was risky," Jack said, "but I did it anyway."

Then he recalled the words his father once told him: "Son, I'm sixty-two now. I've been making decisions all my life. What percent of those decisions do you suppose were good decisions?" Jack figured maybe 40 to 45 percent of his father's decisions were good ones. "Son, that's high. I'm lucky if even 33 percent of my decisions turn out right.

"I'm old enough now that if I wanted to," his father added, "I could just stop making decisions. But if I stopped, that percentage would never change. It would stay at 33 percent until I die.

"Son, you can stop making decisions right now if you want to. If you do, you'll never get above where you are right now. But if you keep on making decisions—even when you're scared—you've got a chance to raise that average. And remember, you normally make better decisions as you get older because you have more experience in life."

That story illustrates a great principle. In Ecclesiastes 11:1–2, Solomon, who has looked at all the problems of the world, now challenges his readers to grab hold of life and take a few chances. Disaster is still just around the corner, but since you can't know how or when or even if it will come, your best course is to "cast your bread upon the waters"; that is, be diligent in your labors so that you may profit from them later.

Nothing has changed in Solomon's overall philosophy: He believes life itself is fleeting and frustrating. But as he begins to wrap up his journey toward reality, his tone seems to change. He's more upbeat, more positive, more encouraging of aggressive action.

Where there is no risk, there is no reward. As the apostle Paul wrote, "Whatever a man sows, this he will also reap" (Galatians 6:7 NASB). But if you never sow the seed, you never reap the harvest. In that case, you are like the man who hid his talent in the ground (Matthew 25:14–30).

All of us go through life making decisions every day. You can take no chances and stay right where you are. Or you can take a few chances and, like Jack's father, maybe raise your average. The choice is up to you.

Lord God, increase my courage so that I may take advantage of every legitimate opportunity that comes my way. Amen.

—✳—

SHINING THE LIGHT

✳ In what areas of your life have you been afraid to move forward for fear of failure? What steps of faith could you take in the next week?

✳ How would your life be different if you began to confront your fears?

—✳—

MORE LIGHT FROM GOD'S WORD

Read Psalm 56:11; Isaiah 43:1–2; and 2 Timothy 1:7.

✳

Eighty-Eight

BOLDNESS: TAKING ADVANTAGE OF EVERY OPPORTUNITY

If clouds are full of water, they pour rain upon the earth.
Whether a tree falls to the south or to the north, in the place
where it falls, there will it lie. Whoever watches the wind
will not plant; whoever looks at the clouds will not reap.

Ecclesiastes 11:3–4

Do you think Solomon was a pessimist? Certainly some of his earlier comments about the calamities of life might be taken that way. He knows full well that the "best laid plans of mice and men" often go astray. Things don't always work out right—they sometimes don't work out at all. Blades grow dull, snakes bite people, walls collapse, the wicked triumph over the righteous, and death comes to all of us sooner or later, sometimes when we least expect it.

This is life as we experience it. What are you going to do? Shrug your shoulders and give up? Stay in bed? Pout about the frowning face of providence?

Consider the dark clouds that mean a storm is advancing over the horizon. The same storm that washes away coastal homes also brings needed rain to the farmer's crops. If the uncertainty of life makes you stay curled up under the covers, you've missed Solomon's point. While it's true that you may be wiped out tomorrow, it's also true that you may strike oil. You'll never know unless you dig another well. But one thing is sure—if you don't dig, you'll never find oil. If you don't plant, you'll never reap the harvest.

Perhaps you've heard the old proverb, "A watched pot never boils." You've got to run some risks to get ahead in the world. Some plans will fail, some crops won't grow, some sales calls won't pan out—so what? Others will succeed, you'll have more watermelons than you know what to do with, and you'll bag the largest order in the history of your company.

The biblical view comes down to this: Since God alone knows the future, we ought to make our plans, use our brains, study the situation, take all factors into consideration, seek wise counsel, do the best we can, and then leave the results to God. Don't be reckless—that's the path of certain ruin; but don't sit on your hands either. Pay your money, take your chances, sleep like a baby, and let God take care of the future.

Lord Jesus, when I am tempted to look at my circumstances and despair, help me to remember that You calmed the storms before and You can do it again. Amen.

— ✳ —

SHINING THE LIGHT

✳ How well do you handle failure? What lessons have you learned from your past mistakes?

✳ Are you gun-shy about the future? If so, what needs to change in your own heart before you can be bold again?

— ✳ —

MORE LIGHT FROM GOD'S WORD

Read Psalm 48:14; Mark 4:35–41; and 2 Corinthians 9:8.

✳

Eighty-Nine

GET BUSY ... NOW!

As you do not know the path of the wind, or how the body is formed in a mother's womb, so you cannot understand the work of God, the Maker of all things. Sow your seed in the morning, and at evening let not your hands be idle, for you do not know which will succeed, whether this or that, or whether both will do equally well.

Ecclesiastes 11:5–6

Life is uncertain. So what? Solomon argues in favor of bold action precisely because you don't know what might happen tomorrow. Get up early, he says, and stay up late. Don't veg in front of the TV. Take every opportunity God gives you and make the best of it.

This practical advice reminds me of a friend who could do it all—sing, teach, lead music; he was a whiz at construction and knew how to fix cars, plus he had attended seminary. One day I asked him about his future. Did he want to be a pastor or teacher or enter some other vocation? Did he hope to get married? He answered that he had run into one of his old seminary professors recently and asked him for some advice. "You're suffering from the curse of too many options," the professor told him.

That's the problem of people who feel like they have too many choices and therefore don't know which way to go. The professor had been raised on a farm and when he graduated from high school, he could have either stayed on the farm or gone to college. So he went to college. When he graduated, he could have either gone back to the farm or to seminary. So he went to seminary. When he graduated, he had no choices, so he went to graduate school. His only job offer came from the seminary he attended, so he took it and remains on the faculty to this day.

"Most people dream of having more options, but I have been blessed by having almost none at all," the professor said. "At each stage of my life, I generally have had only one choice to make, so I made it and kept moving ahead." Solomon would heartily agree with that philosophy.

Would you like to know the "secret" to knowing God's will? If there is a "secret" to be found, it is in doing today what you already know to be God's will. Just get up, get out of bed, take a shower, put on your clothes, eat breakfast, and do what has to be done. As you do God's will today, you will discover God's will for tomorrow.

The moral of the story: Don't worry about your options. Serve the Lord today and tomorrow will take care of itself.

Father, save me from the folly of idle speculation about tomorrow when I should be busy doing my job today. Amen.

—✳—
SHINING THE LIGHT

✳ What project, dream, idea, or initiative have you been postponing? When do you plan to get started?

✳ What's the first step you need to take? So what are you waiting for?

—✳—
MORE LIGHT FROM GOD'S WORD

Read Joshua 6:1–5; Psalm 139:13–16; and 1 Corinthians 15:58.

Ninety

✳

GOD IS IN THE DETAILS

Light is sweet, and it pleases the eyes to see the sun. However many years a man may live, let him enjoy them all. But let him remember the days of darkness, for they will be many. Everything to come is meaningless.

Ecclesiastes 11:7–8

Every day above ground is a bonus." A friend said that last night and I listened carefully because he has just survived difficult surgery to replace a heart valve. Life is good and light is sweet, especially when you've dodged the proverbial bullet and gained a few extra years.

To paraphrase Solomon in Ecclesiastes 11:7–8, "Enjoy life, because you're going to be dead a lot longer than you're going to be alive." A morbid thought, perhaps, but one that no human experience can contradict.

Here's a crucial observation as we apply this truth: About 99 percent of life is ordinary. Many of us struggle with that truth, because we secretly dream of a life of perpetual excitement and unending happiness. A man takes a new job with high hopes and big dreams, only to find that most of his days are filled with the same things he's been doing for the last five years. Or a young woman dreams of a happy married life where she can prepare beautiful dinners and take leisurely strolls with her husband. In her eyes the future seems bright and free from difficulty. But soon enough she discovers that her husband can be grouchy and unappreciative of her most creative culinary efforts. Add to that dirty diapers, a living room that needs straightening four times a day, wet snowsuits, runny noses, dirty hands, and a sink that drips twenty-four hours a day.

Life is more than fun and games. It's also cleaning the oven, paying the bills, and doing the laundry.

Let's face it. Most of our days will be spent doing the "busywork" of life. We get up, get dressed, get the kids ready, eat breakfast, go to work (or to school), see people, attend meetings, answer questions, fill out forms, type letters, make phone calls, review files, make notes, keep appointments, clear our desk, go home, unwind, eat supper, walk the dog, talk to the children, watch TV, and go to bed. Then we get up the next morning and do it again.

Such is life. A great deal of what we do every day may seem mundane and even trivial, but that's where the will of God begins for you and me. Blessed is that man who enjoys the routine, blessed is that woman who delights in the mundane, for they shall discover that God is in the details of life.

Sovereign Lord, open my eyes that I might see how blessed I really am. Amen.

— ✳ —

SHINING THE LIGHT

✳ Think of the three most joyful people you know. What qualities do they share in common?

✳ Take sixty seconds and count your blessings. Then thank God for them.

— ✳ —

MORE LIGHT FROM GOD'S WORD

Read Psalm 90; Ephesians 5:15–17; and Colossians 3:17.

✳

Ninety-One

GOD'S WORD TO PARTY ANIMALS

Be happy, young man, while you are young, and let your heart give you joy in the days of your youth. Follow the ways of your heart and whatever your eyes see, but know that for all these things God will bring you to judgment. So then, banish anxiety from your heart and cast off the troubles of your body, for youth and vigor are meaningless.

Ecclesiastes 11:9–10

Sheila (not her real name) became a widow several years ago. She takes pride in her appearance and has a very pleasant personality. Even a casual observer would understand that she likes and appreciates the finer things of life. The little things give it away—her clothes, the way she carries herself, her conversation, the car she drives.

In the years since her husband's death she has never seriously dated anyone. No interest, not the right kind of men, plenty of things to keep her busy, lots of friends to spend time with. "What would I want with another man in my life?" she says, not meaning to ask a question, really, but simply stating a fact.

Not long ago she went to a wedding where some old family friends introduced her to a man from out of town. He was charming, witty, and great fun.

The next day they, along with two other couples,

went for a boat ride on the river. They laughed, talked, ate fried chicken, and generally had a ball. Afterwards, it was off to a nice restaurant at the marina.

Finally, the evening was almost over. One of the couples loaned the new man their car so he could take Sheila home. When they arrived at her house, they went inside, talked a bit, and then the man asked a question.

"Can you get pregnant?" The lady was shocked but recovered in time to say no. His next question got right to the point, "Do you mind if I sleep here tonight?" This time her answer was quick, almost, she told me later, in the same tone as she speaks to her children, "Oh no, I couldn't do that." He left and has not called her since.

When telling me the story later, Sheila commented, "I could never do what he was asking. I would feel guilty the rest of my life."

There are two quick morals to this little tale. First, no one ever outgrows temptation; that Sheila was an older woman did not matter. Temptation may come in different forms, but come it will. If ever you let down your guard, in that moment Satan will find your weakness and trap you. Second, the best way to defeat temptation is to refuse to take the tiniest step in a wrong direction. Let others stutter and stammer and flirt with danger. Remember the two-letter word that starts with *n* and ends with *o*. It can get you out of trouble and save you from enormous heartache. When temptation comes knocking at your door, just say *no*.

Father, help me to make wise choices today so that a guilty conscience will not keep me awake tonight. Amen.

——*——

SHINING THE LIGHT

* To what extent does the pursuit of pleasure characterize life in our society? Examples, please!

* If being a party animal doesn't really satisfy, why do so many people keep looking there? What happens when we make personal pleasure the ultimate goal of life?

——*——

MORE LIGHT FROM GOD'S WORD

Read Psalm 33:1–3; 1 Corinthians 10:31; and Titus 2:11–14.

✳

Ninety-Two

REMEMBER YOUR CREATOR

Remember your Creator in the days of your youth, before the days of trouble come and the years approach when you will say, "I find no pleasure in them"—before the sun and the light and the moon and the stars grow dark, and the clouds return after the rain.

Ecclesiastes 12:1–2

Have you ever stopped to consider how many young people in the Bible did something significant for God?

- Joseph, sold into slavery at age seventeen by his brothers, rose to become one of the rulers of Egypt and later saved his people in a time of famine (Genesis 37).
- Gideon was just a young man when the Lord used him to rescue Israel from the Midianites (Judges 6–7).
- David was a teenager tending his father's sheep on the hillsides of Bethlehem when he rose up and slew Goliath (1 Samuel 16–17).
- Joash became king of Judah at age seven; he reigned for forty years and led the people in a major refurbishing of the Temple (2 Kings 12).
- Uzziah became king of Judah when he was sixteen years old; he reigned for fifty-two years and was counted as one of the great military leaders of the Bible. At

one point, he led an army of 307,500 fighting men (2 Chronicles 26).

- Hezekiah became king of Judah at the young age of twenty-five and was Judah's greatest king; he reigned for thirty-one years (2 Kings 18–20).
- Josiah became king of Judah when he was only eight years old; he reigned for forty years and led the nation in a mighty religious revival (2 Kings 22–23).
- Daniel was taken captive as a teenager by the Babylonian king Nebuchadnezzar. God honored Daniel's convictions, and he entered the king's service (Daniel 1).

The point must not be missed: God has always used young people to get His message to the world. He still does today. As I think about the next generation of Christian teenagers, I wish I could guarantee them a long life and much happiness. But I can't promise them that. If they decide to live by faith, there are no guarantees. Some of them may not live for seventy years. Some of them may be called of God to serve Christ halfway around the world. Some of them may end up great heroes of the faith; some of them may end up among those who suffer for Jesus Christ.

To any teens and young adults reading these words, I cannot promise you an easy road if you decide to follow Jesus Christ. But I do promise this: If you "remember your Creator in the days of your youth," you will be blessed and you won't be sorry. You will discover that the life of faith is full of adventure, and you will be glad you weren't a couch potato but dared to make a difference in the world.

> *Lord, I don't want to remember You only when I'm dying. Help me to do it now, while it matters, and for the rest of my life. Amen.*

— ✳ —

SHINING THE LIGHT

✳ What does it mean to you to say that God is your creator?

✳ What would it look like if you were to truly "remember" God this week? In what areas are you most tempted to "forget" the Lord?

— ✳ —

MORE LIGHT FROM GOD'S WORD

Read Deuteronomy 8:17–18; Matthew 6:33; and Romans 12:1–2.

------------ ✳ ------------

Ninety-Three

THE BUDDING OF THE ALMOND TREE

When the keepers of the house tremble, and the strong men stoop, when the grinders cease because they are few, and those looking through the windows grow dim; when the doors to the street are closed and the sound of grinding fades; when men rise up at the sound of birds, but all their songs grow faint; when men are afraid of heights and of dangers in the streets; when the almond tree blossoms and the grasshopper drags himself along and desire no longer is stirred. Then man goes to his eternal home and mourners go about the streets.

Ecclesiastes 12:3–5

M any—OK, perhaps most—of us don't like to think about growing older. The hands tremble, the back begins to stoop, our teeth don't work so well, and our eyesight grows dim. We wake up early but don't have the energy we once had. We worry about things that never bothered us before. Sexual ardor fades away. Life itself slows to a crawl.

The words of Ecclesiastes 12:3–5 describe in poetic language the toll that old age takes on the human body. Finally death comes, and man "goes to his eternal home" while his friends gather at his wake to tell a few stories and shed a few tears.

We may not wish to consider our later years, yet this

is life as it really is—this is what is ahead for all of us if we live long enough. The only people who escape this slow decline are those who die before they grow old. The rest of us will learn the truth of Solomon's words. I'm thinking as I write this of a friend of mine who uses a walker to get around because her legs are unsteady. Looking me straight in the eye, she proclaimed, "It's heck growing older." I did not doubt her at all.

There is another side to the story. Psalm 92:12–15 speaks of the vitality of the righteous in their old age. The righteous are blessed with long life and good health and fruitfulness even into old age. They don't dry up and wither away, but bear fruit until the end.

They leave this world, praising God all the way. They proclaim, "The Lord is upright; he is my Rock, and there is no wickedness in him" (Psalm 92:15). Only those who have seen life in all its fullness can say that with conviction. Here is a fundamental difference between the old and the young. The young know the words to the song; the old know the composer.

Perhaps you've heard the story of the young pastor who rose to preach on Psalm 23. He gave it his best effort but never connected with the audience. Afterward an old man got up to speak. He bowed his head, his hands quivering, his body worn from years of hard work. Gripping the podium, he began to recite, "The Lord is my shepherd, I shall not want." As he finished the audience sat in deep silence, profoundly moved. When the young pastor asked the old man why his words had made such a difference, the old man said simply, "You know the psalm, I know the Shepherd."

Some things are learned only through hard experience. Only those who have known suffering and hardship can say with deep conviction, "The Lord is upright. All that He does is good. He makes no mistakes, and He made no mistakes in my life." It is only looking back that the testimony of the righteous is seen in its full power.

> *Lord of years, may all my days be spent serving You and may I come to the end without fear, ready to enter my eternal home through the grace of the Lord Jesus Christ. Amen.*

—✳—

SHINING THE LIGHT

✳ Are you afraid of growing old? Why or why not?

✳ What will happen to you when you die?

—✳—

MORE LIGHT FROM GOD'S WORD
Read John 5:24; 11:25–26; and 1 John 3:1–3.

*

Ninety-Four

A MESSAGE FOR
OLDER SAINTS

Remember him—before the silver cord is severed, or the golden bowl is broken; before the pitcher is shattered at the spring, or the wheel broken at the well, and the dust returns to the ground it came from, and the spirit returns to God who gave it.

Ecclesiastes 12:6–7

Some blessings are given to the young—to marry, give birth, and raise a family for the glory of God, to set out to conquer the world, to find a mountain and climb it, to have a career, to rise in your chosen profession, to make a mark with your life. These things occupy the young.

But the old have a different calling. Most of these things they have already done, having persevered through years of struggle, long nights of prayer, seeing their children grow up and go off to school. They have found satisfying careers, developed lasting friendships, and have a raft of memories that uniquely define who they are. Some have lived so long that they have outlived many of their friends. Perhaps they buried a husband or wife along the way.

God gives to those in the sunset years a unique privilege. At the age of forty-five I can testify only to my life so far. But the elderly have lived far longer and they know from experience things I have not yet discovered.

If you live long enough, you may say, as did the senior in the previous entry, "The Lord is upright. All that He does is good. He makes no mistakes." Perhaps you will be able to add some other personal testimony: "I have seen all that life has to offer, I have known joy and I have known sorrow. My Lord is a Solid Rock and I'm still standing on that Rock. My feet are planted on a firm foundation because the Rock Himself is holding me up.

"I've been battered, bruised, bumped, and done my share of bleeding. I've wept an ocean of tears and learned to laugh afterwards. I've known more than my share of setbacks and difficulties. I know how hard life can be. But the Rock of my Salvation has never failed, never moved, never trembled, for all these years; He has never sagged under the weight of all my problems."

Here is a worthy goal for those who have lived to see the crowning years of life. Do not go silently into the night. Do not let these precious days go by quietly. Speak up for the Lord. We need you more than you know. We need your testimony, your years of experience, and most of all, we need you to tell us, and tell us again, that the Lord is a Rock upon whom we can all rest. Help us fix our lives on the one Rock that cannot be moved. Show us the way and someday we will thank you by sharing with our children what you have told us.

Rock of Ages, grant that my faith may remain strong until I draw my dying breath and go home to be with Jesus. Amen.

— ✳ —

SHINING THE LIGHT

✳ Think of the last person you knew who died unexpectedly. What lessons do you draw from that person's life and death?

✳ If you were to die today, what three things would your friends and family remember most about you?

— ✳ —

MORE LIGHT FROM GOD'S WORD

Read Genesis 3:19; Job 1:20–21; and 1 Thessalonians 4:13–18.

✳

Ninety-Five

NAILS FROM THE SHEPHERD

"Meaningless! Meaningless!" says the Teacher. "Everything is meaningless!" Not only was the Teacher wise, but also he imparted knowledge to the people. He pondered and searched out and set in order many proverbs. The Teacher searched to find just the right words, and what he wrote was upright and true. The words of the wise are like goads, their collected sayings like firmly embedded nails—given by one Shepherd.

Ecclesiastes 12:8–11

The experiment has ended. With the words "meaningless, meaningless," Solomon ends where he began—with the utter vanity of life apart from God. Taking the standpoint of a man "under the sun," he has searched every possible avenue to find the key to the meaning of life. His search led him to wealth, wisdom, education, pleasure, possessions, achievement, fame, folly, and eventually to the house of sorrow. He examined it all and discovered that without God, life is truly meaningless.

No matter what you accomplish in this life, death trumps everything else. Since we all die and no one knows what happens afterwards, nothing is left but to enjoy the short life God gives you.

The last few verses of Ecclesiastes 12 are Solomon's

personal epilogue to the reader. They summarize the journey and apply the truth to the human heart. Verse 11 reminds us that Solomon's wisdom came from God. They also tell us how hard he worked to write this short book—how he arranged the stories and proverbs to produce a pleasing result.

We also discover why he wrote as he did. His words are like sharp goads—meant to stick in the mind. If you find yourself arguing with something in Ecclesiastes, all the better, because Solomon fully intended to nail the truth to your heart. His is no mere devotional book, meant to be picked up and read casually. To the contrary, only serious readers will appreciate his literary creation.

Solomon himself acknowledged the wisdom contained in the book came from God—the "one Shepherd" (verse 11). This should answer forever those critics and commentators who doubt the value and inspiration of Ecclesiastes. The same Shepherd who gave Romans to Paul gave Ecclesiastes to Solomon.

This brings us face-to-face with the inspiration of Holy Scripture. No question could be more fundamental. Christians believe and teach that the Bible alone is the Word of God. When the Bible speaks, God speaks. What the Bible says, God says.

The Bible stands alone because it was given by one Shepherd to many authors over 1,500 years. No other book can remotely be compared to it. No one who reads it with an open mind will ever be disappointed.

O God of truth, I thank You for the Holy Scriptures, for in them I discover the way to life eternal. May the truth of Your Word be etched on the tablets of my heart. Amen.

———✳———

SHINING THE LIGHT

✳ What does it mean to you to say that the Bible is the Word of God?

✳ What "nails" of truth have you gained from this study of Ecclesiastes? Which passages were like "goads" that seemed to stick in your mind?

———✳———

MORE LIGHT FROM GOD'S WORD

Read Psalm 119:105; 2 Timothy 3:16–17; and Hebrews 4:12–13.

Ninety-Six

MAKE UP YOUR MIND!

Be warned, my son, of anything in addition to them. Of making many books there is no end, and much study wearies the body.

Ecclesiastes 12:12

As a careful reading of Ecclesiastes makes clear, Solomon enjoyed the challenge of mastering a new topic. He didn't mind doing the hard work of research necessary in order to find the truth. But eventually the time comes when you have to make up your mind. You can't sit on the fence forever. If your studies don't lead you to the Lord, then perhaps you've been studying the wrong things.

It meant taking a long motorcycle ride over the dusty, hot roads of northern India, but I jumped at the chance to see the actual village work. When we arrived in a small village in the state of Bihar, my guide introduced me to two local Christian leaders. Together we sat down on the mat and I listened with awe as the two men sang original songs they had written in the local dialect of the Hindi language. Indian music sounds nothing at all like Western music—the pitch, tone, and rhythms are completely different. But they sang with enthusiasm and obvious joy in the Lord, accompanied only by a tambourine that one man beat against his shin.

The leader of the local congregation came from a warrior caste. His people had a long and proud history that stretched back many centuries. How did he become a Christian? It started a few years ago when someone told him about the Bible. Although he was illiterate, he tried to read it, and as he did a light shined from heaven upon Matthew 5:5 and gave him the meaning. This miraculous insight appeared to him several more times, each time teaching him more about Jesus.

When he finally accepted Christ, his wife threw him out of their house, whereupon he moved to this village and joined the small band of believers. With great pride he showed me the stones in the ground for the new church they hoped to build. It wasn't large—about 11 feet by 17 feet—but his face glowed with joy at the thought of having a proper building for God's worship.

Through a translator he told me five other men in this village had a name identical to his. Therefore, his official address consists of his name plus the word "Christian," because he was the only believer by that name in the village.

Although it's not easy for him to be known as Mr. Christian, he smiled as he told me the story. He thinks that God is going to do something great in his village. I believe he's right, because God honors those who aren't ashamed of Jesus' name.

Lord, I ask for the courage to make up my mind, so that I won't be guilty of always searching but never quite finding the way of truth. Amen.

— ✳ —

SHINING THE LIGHT

✳ Name someone you know who is "sitting on the fence" spiritually. What will it take to move the person to a decision one way or the other?

✳ In what areas of your life do you need to make up your mind? What is holding you back?

— ✳ —

MORE LIGHT FROM GOD'S WORD

Read Psalm 119:89–91; John 17:17; and 2 Timothy 3:6–7.

✳

Ninety-Seven

THE LAST WORD AND
THE FIRST RULE

*Now all has been heard; here is the conclusion of the matter:
Fear God and keep his commandments, for this is the whole
duty of man.*

Ecclesiastes 12:13

Where can we find meaning in life? Answer: Life makes sense if you fear God and keep His commandments. And conversely, nothing makes sense if you don't. If life is like a long, dark tunnel, then this is the light at the end.

Fear God! Keep His commandments! This is your whole duty. This is why you were born. Everything else is just details. That is Solomon's conclusion at the end of his journey to find ultimate meaning.

Several weeks ago a friend e-mailed me with the news that his mother's cancer surgery had been successful. He ended his message with this statement: "God is God, good, and great." As I pondered his words, I was struck at once by their simplicity and profundity. How much truth those six little words contain. They summarize an entire Christian worldview.

To say that God is God is simply to remind ourselves of the First Rule of the Spiritual Life: He's God and we're not. When I read my Bible it seems to pop up on every page and in every biblical story. Because God is God, He does whatever pleases Him and works in every situation of life in ways I cannot see and would not understand if I could see. This is a humbling truth because it brings me to my knees and forces me to admit that God alone is running the universe and I'm not running any part of it—not even the part I think I'm running.

To say that God is good means that His heart is inclined toward kindness. This gives me courage to pray for mercy in times of trouble. It also helps me to keep a positive perspective when life tumbles in around me. We often say that all things work together for good—and they do (Romans 8:28)—but that's true only because God Himself is good. That means I can be content right now because I have everything I need at any given moment. If I truly needed anything else, God would give it to me.

To say that God is great means that He isn't limited by my circumstances but can work through them for my good and His glory.

Let these six simple words lift your spirits: "God is God, good, and great." God is God; be humbled. God is good; be encouraged. God is great; be thankful. Center your life on Him and in the end you will have no regrets.

Almighty God, to know You is life's highest goal and the reason for which I was created. May I be satisfied with nothing less. Amen.

—✳—

SHINING THE LIGHT

✳ What does it mean to fear God? What are the marks of a person who fears God?

✳ Why is this the first step in the spiritual life?

—✳—

MORE LIGHT FROM GOD'S WORD

Read 1 Samuel 12:24; Proverbs 9:10; and Hebrews 12:1–3.

Ninety-Eight

CORAM DEO

*For God will bring every deed into judgment, including
every hidden thing, whether it is good or evil.*

Ecclesiastes 12:14

Solomon's final argument in favor of serving God may
come as a surprise. Instead of ending on an "up" note,
he reminds us one final time of the coming day of judgment when our lives will pass under His all-seeing eyes.
This means that everything we do and say is important.
Since nothing is hidden, everything ultimately matters.

I know many people who struggle with questions of
right and wrong—especially in those areas for which we
have no explicit guidance in the Bible. They truly want to
please the Lord, but worry about their daily decisions.
Here is a simple question that will replace many of the
dos and don'ts: Can I do this to God's glory? That is, if I
do this, will it enhance God's reputation in the world?
Will those who watch me know that I know God from
my behavior? Or will I simply have to explain this away
or apologize for it later?

That brings us back to Question 1 of the Westminster Shorter Catechism: What is the chief purpose of
man? "To glorify God and enjoy Him forever." We were
made to glorify God. Nothing works right when we

don't.

In putting the matter this way I am calling for nothing less than a God-centered life. That means intentionally making your decisions so that God's reputation is enhanced in the world. The Puritans often used the Latin phrase *coram Deo*, which means "under the face of God." It's a reminder that God is always watching everything we do. His eye is always on us, nothing escapes His notice, and all of life must be lived for His approval.

J. S. Bach carved the words *Soli Deo Gloria* on his organ at Leipzig, Germany, to remind him that all his music be composed and performed for the glory of God. The initials SDG appear at the end of his compositions: "To God alone be the glory." That's what I mean by intentional God-centered living.

All I am saying may be summed up this way. People watch what we do and say and draw huge conclusions from our tiniest personal decisions. Living in the light of God's glory means to live so that others will draw the right conclusions as they watch us.

Ruth Bell Graham defines a saint this way: "A saint is someone who makes it easy to believe in Jesus." May God help us to live that way every day.

> *Righteous Judge, help to me to live in such a way that I will not be ashamed when I stand before You. Amen.*

—✳—

SHINING THE LIGHT

✳ Name three practical ways you can glorify God this week.

✳ How does it make you feel to know that God is watching you this very moment? Is there anything in your life that you would be ashamed for God to bring to light when you stand before Him?

—✳—

MORE LIGHT FROM GOD'S WORD

Read Romans 14:9–12; 2 Corinthians 5:10; and 1 John 2:28.

Ninety-Nine

THE TRUEST BOOK IN THE BIBLE

"Meaningless! Meaningless!" says the Teacher. "Utterly meaningless! Everything is meaningless." . . . Now all has been heard; here is the conclusion of the matter: Fear God and keep his commandments, for this is the whole duty of man.

Ecclesiastes 1:2; 12:13

When I set out to write this book, several of my friends wondered whether this was a worthwhile project. A number commented on how rarely they had read Ecclesiastes. At least one person cautioned that Ecclesiastes could not be trusted because Solomon wrote it in a spiritually backslidden condition.

My viewpoint is almost entirely the opposite. It seems to me that Ecclesiastes is the truest book in the Bible. I doubt that I would have said that twenty years ago—on reflection, I know that I wouldn't have—because I simply didn't appreciate the depth of Solomon's brutal candor about the ragged edges of life. Over the years, this book has become more and more familiar to me until at last it seems as natural and honest as anything in the Bible.

Not long ago I commented to my congregation that

as a pastor I am very weary of doing funerals. After two decades of visiting mortuaries and doing graveside services, I have seen all the death I ever want to see. I've done funerals for babies, for young people, for adults who died suddenly, and many services for older people who died after a long illness. It's not that I don't find a profound satisfaction in bringing God's comfort to grieving hearts. I do, and I thank God for calling me into the ministry. But of death itself I am very tired. I long to see a few resurrections. In feeling that way, I am in good company because Solomon struggled mightily with the awesome reality of human death.

But I know something Solomon never knew. I know that Jesus Christ has come back from the dead. There is no other reason to think that we will ever see our loved ones again. The New Testament again and again connects our resurrection with His. Ours will happen in the future because His happened in the past. Sometimes when I stand by the grave of someone I know, I can almost hear a voice from beneath the ground saying, "I'm coming up." To unbelievers that may sound like wishful thinking, but to me it's nothing but solid biblical faith. In the words of the Apostles' Creed, I believe in the resurrection of the dead.

Ecclesiastes is true and when it comes to the human condition, this may be the truest book in the Bible. But it's not the final word.

Lord Jesus, thank You for solid answers to life's hardest questions. Amen.

—✳—

SHINING THE LIGHT

✳ Which parts of Ecclesiastes are hardest for you to understand? Which parts seem to ring true to your own experience?

✳ Do you believe in the resurrection of the dead?

—✳—

MORE LIGHT FROM GOD'S WORD

Read Psalm 111; Romans 8:31–35; and Revelation 19:1–5.

*

SOLOMON AND JESUS

I became greater by far than anyone in Jerusalem before me. In all this my wisdom stayed with me. . . . "The Queen of the South will rise at the judgment with the men of this generation and condemn them; for she came from the ends of the earth to listen to Solomon's wisdom, and now one greater than Solomon is here."

Ecclesiastes 2:9; Luke 11:31

Jesus mentioned Solomon twice. In the first instance He commented that Solomon in all his glory did not possess the simple glory of the lilies of the field (see Matthew 6:29; Luke 12:27). The lilies don't even work for what they have. God gives it to them. And do you think the flowers worry? The flowers don't even last very long. You buy some today and by Wednesday they've started to wilt. Little helpless flowers that pass away so quickly. Yet God takes care of them.

But we are not flowers. We are living souls. Your body is not you. It's part of you, but it's not the whole you. The real you is more than the sum total of your blood, muscles, bones, fat, nerves, and skin. You are not just a piece of gross anatomy. You are a living soul in a body made by God. And you are going to live forever somewhere. That's makes you infinitely more valuable than the lilies of the field. And it actually puts you in a better position than Solomon if you understand that God has promised to take care of you.

Jesus' only other mention of Solomon occurs in a context of judgment on the wicked generation that rejected Him (see Matthew 12:42; Luke 11:31). The Queen of Sheba came hundreds of miles to learn from Solomon (1 Kings 10:1–13) and left mightily impressed with his wisdom. Yet Jesus was greater than Solomon and people rejected Him. Matthew Henry points out that the queen came a long way yet Christ is in our midst. She had no invitation but we are invited to sit at Jesus' feet. Solomon had wisdom from God, but Christ is the wisdom of God. The queen could only learn wisdom from Solomon, but Christ can give wisdom to all who ask for it. Henry concludes that if we do not receive Christ's wisdom, then the Queen of Sheba will rise up in judgment against us, "for Jesus is greater than Solomon."

With that statement our journey ends where life begins—with Jesus Christ.

Lord God, forgive me for looking anywhere else for satisfaction. May my cry always be, Only Jesus and Jesus only! Amen.

——✶——

SHINING THE LIGHT

✶ How is Jesus greater than Solomon?

✶ In what ways are you currently receiving the wisdom of Christ? What is the condition of your heart?

——✶——

MORE LIGHT FROM GOD'S WORD

Read Isaiah 9:6–7; Ephesians 4:20–24; and Hebrews 1:1–3.